Soul-Healing Love is a good balance of spiritual, psychological, and relational information that is practical yet powerful for hurting individuals, couples, and families.

— **Professor Andrew Chung, University of Seoul Korea**

Soul-Healing Love provides a road map for a couple's spiritual journey. It gives guidance for transforming struggles into sacredness and fear into faith. The tools and techniques you will learn will give you the answers you seek and the solutions you need to create a loving relationship. This book should be on the nightstand of every couple.

— **Dr. Patricia Love, Speaker and Author of the Truth About Love, Austin, TX.**

The Rodgers offer a unique combination of practical skills and spiritual insight that helps couples and individuals bring Agape love and deeper commitment to their relationships. I heartily endorse their ministry.

— **Rev. David Chadwick, Veteran Pastor, Forest Hills Presbyterian Church, Charlotte, NC and Radio Talk Show Host**

Drs. Tom and Bev Rodgers have written a remarkably relatable book for couples. Discovering and healing old hurts can be very difficult for some people. Soul Healing Love makes this process much easier. This book is written with candor and sincerity, by real people who openly share their own struggles as well as those of their clients. Immense healing can take place individually and as a couple if you follow the model, and you won't be condemned to repeat the same mistakes the generations before you did. You will also see that being soul mates is truly attainable!

> — Eric and Jennifer Garcia, Co-Founders Association of Marriage and Family Ministries (AMFM)

The Rodgers' Soul Healing Love details how the basic biblical principles of patience, love and forgiveness really work in healing even the most broken of marriages. They have the know how to help couples succeed!

> — Mark Gungor, Christian Comedian

"Tom and Bev Rodgers understand the importance of soul-healing love being lived out in the lives of couples who desire a covenant marriage. One of the greatest factors of a covenant marriage is that of being a spouse who is willing to stand between anything or anyone who seeks to harm the one you love. Soul-healing love requires that we be willing to lay down our life for our covenant partner."

> — Phil Waugh is the Director of Covenant Marriage Movement

Soul-Healing Love

*Turning Relationships that Hurt into
Relationships that Heal*

Soul-Healing Love

Turning Relationships that Hurt into
Relationships that Heal

Drs. Beverly and Tom Rodgers

Printed in Canada

Publishing services by Selah Publishing Group, LLC, Arizona. The views expressed or implied in this work do not necessarily reflect those of Selah Publishing Group.

ISBN: 978-1-58930-177-1
Library of Congress Control Number: 2006907406

Contents

Introduction

*A*s Christian marriage counselors for the past two and a half decades, and as a married couple for some thirty years, we never set out to develop a model of relationships or marriage counseling. All we wanted to do was heal our own hurting marriage. Unlike many of the Christian friends we envied, we did not come from a long line of stable marriages. In fact, both of us came from divorced homes that had deeply wounded us and caused us many problems in our marriage. We entered into marriage fearful of divorce and devoid of healthy role models to teach us the skills to be successful.

Our parent's divorces were not the only demons in our marriage. We both came from homes where we were emotionally and verbally abused. I (Bev) came from severe physical abuse, as well. These scars set us up to have a very difficult time doing marriage successfully, and we did not even know it.

Tom and I did everything we could to deal with the wounds that haunted us in our relationship. We thought that being strong Christians would immunize us against the hurt from our dysfunctional families of origin. We seriously took to heart the scripture 2 Corinthians 5:17: "Therefore, if anyone is in Christ, he is a new creation; the old has gone, the new has come!" (NIV). We literally thought that "old things" would pass away and that we would not even remember the hurtful events of childhood, much less allow them to affect us in our adult lives. Little did we know what would lie ahead for these well-meaning, naïve honeymooners.

We also thought that if being a Christian was not enough, we would get advanced degrees in religion and psychology in order to approach healing our soul wounds from both angles. It was our belief that studying these areas would inoculate us from feeling the pain of our childhoods. To further our cause, we got advanced degrees in the field of marriage and family counseling, and read as many books as we could on the subject. With all of this, we were sure that we would not suffer the slings and arrows from our past. Unfortunately, this did not happen.

We would do fine until one of us was triggered. The situation could be incidental. You may have similar circumstances in your own relationship. Things between you and your spouse start out benign, then, before you know it, you are in an all-out fight and you are not even sure what caused it. You try to tell yourself that you are overreacting. You may even tell yourself to calm down or even shut up, but to no avail. Your reaction triggers a reaction in your spouse, and now you are both deep in a power struggle.

Without healthy communication tools, you feel stuck. You may be verbal, like Tom was in our early marriage, and yell and threaten, or you may simply pout and become icy like I did. But the results are still the same. You are distant and alone with no resolution in sight. We hated these times in the beginning of our relationship. We've even developed a name for them. We call them "marital purgatory."

In order to find our way out of our dilemma, we attended seminars and workshops on marriage. Although many of them were helpful, they often left us wanting, or more accurately, longing. Many were too superficial, and others were too mystical, touting trite suggestions like "Just trust God." Some seminars seemed downright impossible to replicate for us wounded birds.

I remember one particular theorist who presented his work using himself and his starry-eyed wife to demonstrate his magical communication techniques. There they were—the Barbie and Ken of the marriage counseling scene. She was from an upper-middle-class religious family, and he descended from great Christian orators and philosophers. How inadequate we felt beside these two partners with their great foundations, discussing their ideas of marital bliss. Boy, did we ever feel like fish out of water. Our familial histories of divorce alone were enough to disqualify us from ever achieving this goal of "matrimonial nirvana."

Where, we asked ourselves, were the fearful, neurotic, wounded couples like us? Where were those honest souls, desiring to love and be loved, baggage and all? Where do truly wounded souls go to find intimacy? These are the people we want in a communication seminar—the yellers, the blamers, the pouters, and the icy stonewallers. These are the real men and women of the marital trenches. These wounded souls, with broken dreams from poor role models and sagging foundations from childhood wounds, are the real heroes of the marital battlefield—not Barbie and Ken. These people are the ones who are aware that they are in the midst of a war, thrilling and terrible at the same time. These precious, brave sojourners are the ones we want to see in a marriage workshop—the ones who need to find the strength and resources to love their partner even when it seems too hard.

Yes, Barbie and Ken's ideas are noteworthy, but many of us wounded souls feel that we are crippled, even as we start this journey. We do not know how to deal with intimacy and oneness—and most of the time, it frankly scares us. It was with this fear and desire that we developed the Soul Healing Love Model of marriage, which we are going to outline for you in this book.

The model grew out of our trying (and often failing) to find a way out of the unhealthy conflicts and differences that threatened our marriage. As we began to deal with our own woundedness and see how it affected our marriage, unbeknownst to us, the Lord began to give us a model that started to heal our souls and allow us to be healers for each other. We started using it with our clients, who found great success in healing their ailing marriages, as well. Teaching the Soul Healing Love Model at seminars and workshops became an offshoot of this effort. While it helped couples in crisis, dating and engaged couples also attended our workshops and found it very helpful. Couples who just needed a tune up or a little boost found it enriching, as well.

Now we speak across the globe, sharing the model the Lord has given us with dating, engaged, and happily married couples, as well as those in crisis. We have even had some divorced couples attend our fifteen-hour Intensive Soul Healers Couple's Weekends, and reunite after learning this information. We hear from many that soul healing love is one of the greatest gifts they have ever received. Because we spent so many years in our own marital purgatory, we know exactly what they mean.

The Soul Healing Love Model has as its foundation many other models of relationships and marital counseling. We offer thanks and praise to the theorists who have gone before us and have helped us as a married couple get out of the power struggle and move into the healing light. We also offer gratitude to them professionally for giving us great material and outstanding research to draw from in building this model. But the greatest thanks and praise goes the Lord Jesus Christ for anointing this model and entrusting it to two wounded souls who just wanted to be healed, feel secure in their marriage, and dedicate their lives to healing other couples just like them. For this we are truly grateful to our loving heavenly Father.

Sprinkled throughout this book are case studies of actual couples who have learned to use the Soul Healing Love Model successfully. Their names and details have been altered to protect their anonymity. We are grateful for the faith they have displayed in the model as they trusted us with their sacred souls. These precious couples truly honored us by their participation and success. You, too, honor us as you read through these pages.

Some of you may be reading this book because you have learned to practice soul healing love and you want to teach other couples about it. You might want to start a couple's Bible study, fellowship group, or mentoring program and experience this material together. Soul Healers groups like these are cropping up across the globe as couples learn the tools and techniques with one another. We now have many good teaching aids, workbooks, CDs, and DVDs to help you. You will find them at www.SoulHealingLove.com.

This book was written for you brave souls who desire active duty in the war of love and marriage. And make no mistake—Satan, the enemy of our souls, is at war with us, fighting against the success of our marriages as we speak. We dedicate this book to you warrior couples who still have enough determination, faith, and hope to make your marriage work. For those courageous souls who set sail on this precarious, yet unavoidable voyage, we bid you God's understanding and His infinite wisdom as you read the "map" that lies ahead. Let us journey now, to discover a long-term, heart-satisfying, soul healing love. We are thrilled to have you traveling with us.

CHAPTER 1

THE PURPOSE
OF LOVE

*M*arriages in the United States are crumbling. Even with government monies being dedicated to build lasting marriages, and marital strengthening programs sprouting up in churches, parishes, and community-based organizations across the country, half of all marriages still end in divorce. Unfortunately, this is even true in the Christian community. While this may mean guaranteed work for us as Christian marriage counselors for decades to come, we want to do something to prevent these painful divorces and turn things around for today's couples.

We have all heard a story much like the following one. Fred and Wilma had been married for thirty-three years. Fred was a leader in the community and taught a young couple's Sunday school class for some twenty years. Many young couples looked up to him as an example because of his excellent tutelage on matrimony. Then, suddenly, Fred left his wife and two grown children and moved in with Betty, his twenty-seven-year-old divorced secretary. Wilma begged Fred to come to marriage counseling, but he refused, and their marriage ended.

Ward and June were married for fourteen years and had three beautiful children. But then June suddenly announced that she thought her marriage was suffocating her, and that she was not in love with Ward anymore. She wanted out, and so she left him and the kids and joined an archeological dig in a New Mexico graduate school. Ward continued to come to counseling and bring their children to us for help. We will never forget the pain on their eight-year-old son's face when he said he wanted to die because life as he knew it would never be the same. We still see the children on occasion, and they report that their mom has had several serial relationships with younger men, but she is not happy, and she still does not have the love she wants. As marital therapists, we wonder how this could have been prevented.

Accounts like these send shockwaves throughout people's families, friends, churches, and communities. The ripple effect of such events impacts the community for many seasons to come. Tom and I see these kinds of disheartened lovers every day. They come in all shapes and sizes, and so do their emotional wounds and hurts. But they all share one common characteristic—they desperately want a happy, fulfilling love relationship that lasts, and they just can't seem to find it.

Nowadays, if a couple makes it past twenty-five years of marriage, they are looked upon as heroes or relational icons. Society sees them as unusually lucky, extremely laidback, or just plain deaf, dumb, and blind. When Tom and I flew to New York for our twentieth wedding anniversary, the ticket agent at the airport called his friends over to announce, "Hey, guys, look at this couple! Can you believe that they have been married twenty years, and to the same person no less? They should get first-class seats for accomplishing this." And we did! He and his buddies bumped us up to first class and gave us the royal treatment because they were impressed with our marital commitment.

We wish that marital longevity was the norm in our society. We would have gladly given up our first-class seats on our flight just to have been considered "average." But sadly this is not so. Happy, fulfilling, long-term relationships are becoming more and more rare. Marriage counseling practices are filled with couples who just can't seem to grasp love's magic.

What is this thing called "love" anyway? How do some couples seem to get it right while others stumble from relationship to relationship? Is love just a mystical experience that finds some souls lucky, and leaves others barren and longing? So many songs are sung about love, and movies make romantic love the primary objective of the film. Even after the hero destroys the villain, he still has time to find the love of his life.

Being a perennial romantic, I (Bev) would like to believe that true love would find me worthy of its bounty, and that I would find that mystical love that would heal all of my life's ills and quiet all of my internal pain. Because of this desire, I (along with Tom) have studied love from many aspects, and found that true love is far less mystical or magical than our culture or the media portrays. We have come to a solemn but very real conclusion: True love is hard work!

Long-term, committed love is the hardest work our souls will ever do. Like many other great gifts, it has its sacrifices and its responsibilities. Contrary to what movies, romance novels, and almost-forgotten fairytales have depicted for years, love is not easy. Loving the soul of another human being and receiving his or her love in return is an awesome challenge. It takes insight, fortitude, wisdom, and skill. Love doesn't come magically or all at once. It takes time and patience. "Happily ever after" means arduous effort.

In our Soul Healers Workshops, we often quote from the movie *A League of Their Own,* when Geena Davis, who plays a female baseball player, says she is leaving the team. Tom Hanks, who plays the derelict coach, asks why. "Because it just got too hard," is her answer. We love the coach's comeback: "Of course, it is hard! That's what makes it so great." We tell couples all the time that marriage is hard, and it is precisely that difficulty that makes it great.

So, if love is so hard, why do we want it so badly? The answer is simple. Because we do. Humans are hardwired for love. The greatest need for the human soul is to love and be loved. We all want to feel love's warmth wrap around us. Many of us secretly hunger for it, while others search more overtly. Nevertheless, the goal is still the same—to find true love, to find a love that heals one's soul, to find a love that lasts. While love does have its mystical qualities and is very difficult to understand, we believe that it *is* attainable for all those who bravely knock upon its door.

A Familiar Tale

We remember two, young, naïve college kids some thirty years ago who embarked on this course of long-term love, not knowing where the winds of fortune would take them. Their story may strike a cord of familiarity in many of you. It begins with a young girl growing up in a small, backward southern town. She spent a good bit of her childhood watching her parents' bitter, violent fights. When she went to bed at night she would put her hands over her ears and secretly pray that no one would be seriously maimed, disfigured, or dead when she awoke. Most of the time, she was lucky, but there were a few close calls. Her mother, an adult child of an alcoholic, would scream accusations of indiscretions at her father, who would then retaliate.

When the dust settled in the morning, she would tiptoe through the mangled house, which looked much like the wake of a hurricane, and secretly vow to herself that she would never have a marriage like this. She didn't know how she was going to avoid it, but she was not going to live like those two. This would never happen to her!

Things worsened in her home. Her father finally left her mother, breaking the young girl's heart. Her mom grew hard and bitter. Dad remarried a much younger woman and moved away, making visitations less frequent. Mom went to work fulltime, leaving four latchkey waifs to sail parentless on the sea of the 1960s.

Her brother found peace, love, flower power, and unfortunately, drugs. She found religion. With this newly acquired religion as her bastion of hope, she set out to make things different. She knew this was her answer. God would never let her have a marriage like her parents. His Word spoke of harmony, commitment, fidelity, and unconditional love. With the help of her faith, she would not repeat her parent's mistakes. She would be different. She would find her true love. Her dreams would come true.

On the other side of the United States, in contemporary California, a young boy was having struggles of his own. Being raised in a churchgoing family with a church elder for a father and a Sunday school teacher for a mother, it was devastating for him to discover that his family was breaking up due to his father's chronic adultery. This was the man he had looked up to. This man, whom he had idolized as a child, had disappointed and betrayed him. His family was falling apart, and there was nothing he could do about it. They managed to stay together (for the children's sake) until the boy graduated from college, and then they divorced. Disillusioned and hopeless, the young man set out for redemption through a life of Christian service, vowing deep inside that he would live his life differently. With God's help, he would not repeat his parent's pattern. He, unlike them, would find his life's love. He would find his soul mate.

And so it was that the young hillbilly girl from Tennessee found the contemporary boy from California. His parents divorced after twenty-six years and hers after only eleven, leaving both with the same scars and fears that many grown kids of divorced parents possess. They were both united with the hope and dream that they were going to handle marriage differently from their parents. They were also both very afraid. It was with this hope, and with this fear, that their relationship began.

This story is very familiar to us. The names have been somewhat obscured to protect the innocent—and the guilty. This is our story. Now, some thirty years later, we are still in awe of love's mysteries. We have found love to be both mystical and literal, abstract and concrete, both verb and noun. We are, above all, grateful that it found us worthy of its magnificent rewards. These rewards did not come without a great price, and it is for this reason that we wanted to write this book.

We chose to write about soul healing love, not because we are such a great example of matrimony, but rather because we are not. But despite our family histories of divorce, abuse, and dysfunction, our idiosyncratic personality quirks, and our weird phobic predispositions, we have managed to survive marriage (sometimes just barely) for some thirty years.

Our journey has brought us through moves, career changes, poverty, riches, two beautiful children, several adored pets, and even a frightening brush with death. Currently in mid-life, we have compassion for those who wonder why everything wrinkles, sags, bulges, and generally refuses to function at this stage of life's game. We have felt the infamous loss of energy and life passion that goes with a mid-life crisis. And as marriage and family therapists, we not only see this in each other, but also in our clients.

Now, don't get the wrong idea here. Just because we are both therapists, it does not mean that we have any better edge against the demons of our hurtful pasts. In fact, it can be quite embarrassing to slide into unhealthy, dysfunctional communication patterns when we spend all day instructing others not to do so. Here again we have to say, almost despite ourselves, we have learned from our own experiences, and would like to pass some of this wisdom on to the next generation of lovers.

It is our hope that by sharing these hard lessons learned, we can ease the fear and pain that often accompanies intimacy, and instill the hope in this generation that true love is an attainable reality. We want couples to learn that true love is less magic and more hard work than the media would like us to believe, that falling in love is different from staying in love, and that loving someone means wanting to heal the pain of their soul, as they in turn heal yours. True, soul healing love is possible.

Where Love Starts

In order to understand the design of long-term love, we only have to begin at the beginning. Genesis 2:24–25 describes the institution of marriage: "For this reason a man will leave his father and mother and be united to his wife, and they will become one flesh. The man and his wife were both naked, and they felt no shame" (NIV). This passage gives us a clear idea of what marriage is about. First, men and women are to leave. This leaving is not merely a moving out from under the roof or authority of our previous families in order to establish a new unit. It is also a turning away from our original family's influence and what they have consciously and unconsciously imprinted upon our psyches.

In Scripture we see that marriage is designed in such a way that couples must turn away from the functions and dysfunctions of the past in order to establish a new healing love in marriage. As we move from the joys and scars of the past to this new love, we will cleave to each other. The Hebrew word picture here is talking about soldering, much like a welder would solder two metals together. When the craftsman has completed his final product, the observer cannot discern where one metal alloy leaves off and the other begins.

Synergy

To compliment this illustration, let's look at the term *synergy*. This is a term used more in the context of the field of chemistry rather than in relationships. *Synergy* is defined as the interaction of elements that, when combined, produce a total effect that is greater than the sum of its parts.[1] The true love that God has designed for His children puts the hearts and souls of two individuals together and merges them with a synergistic energy to produce a union that is greater than the sum of its two parts. It is this cleaving that merges human souls into oneness.

This soul-merging oneness is not to be confused with how women in the 1950s found their identity in their husbands, because they did not have a sense of who they were on their own. These women became appendages of men. In this type of oneness, wives' opinions were stated by their husbands, and their roles were dictated by culture and society. Since our culture shined more favorably on men at the time, women found their roles dictated to them, as opposed to having the freedom to choose ways in which they wished to serve in their marriages.

This created a severe identity crisis for many of them. Mutual submission, as discussed in the Ephesians 5 passage, was rarely achieved at this point in the development of marriage. Women with low self-esteems needed identities, and their husbands provided them. While the two were considered "one" (ask her what she thought, and he'd answer), this is not the glorious oneness we speak of in this text.

Codependency and Oneness

This same soul healing oneness is also not to be confused with the codependency that was touted in the 1980s, in which women and men got their self-esteem needs met by over-involving themselves in the needs of others, especially their husbands. Codependents live other people's lives by controlling, enabling, or caretaking. A common example of codependency is the enabling wife of the alcoholic, who lives to make her husband sober, while her very helping leads him to drink more. There's a saying that when the codependent dies, everyone else's life passes before his or her eyes. While a codependent wife thinks that her caretaking love will heal her mate, her low self-esteem and misunderstanding of true oneness create more distance than soul healing.

True Soul Healing Love

True soul healing love is not like the types of relationships described above. Caring for the soul of another, true soul healing love, is neither merging identities nor codependency. It is learning to accept and love ourselves as God does, and then taking that awesome God-given love and acceptance and willingly bestowing it upon our partner. Think for a moment about the love of God. Meditate on the greatness of this gift. God loves us with all of our warts and flaws.

People with soul wounds may believe in their head that God loves them, but they do not feel this love in their hearts. These perplexed souls do not see how God could accept them with all of their defects. As a result, they do not love and accept themselves. These individuals judge themselves harshly and without mercy. Often they judge their partners with the same harshness as well.

Tom and I are two such people. We both had many soul wounds that inhibited us from fully accepting God's unconditional love. In the Soul Healing Love Model, we define a *soul wound* as those hurts and pains inflicted upon the psyche that cause tremendous pain and often leave severe emotional scars. Rejection, abandonment, criticism, abuse, and neglect are types of soul wounds. This subject will be covered more thoroughly in Chapter Three. These hurts cause us to feel inadequate and unworthy of love. It is God's unconditional love that heals these soul wounds. His love restores us to wholeness. This is great news for those of us who were severely wounded as children.

For many years after I (Bev) became a Christian, I could not understand why I was still in such emotional pain because of my past. I thought that I was sentenced to a life of suffering. I then came across a passage of scripture that became a theme for me. It was Jeremiah 30:17: "'For I will restore health to you and heal you of your wounds,' says the LORD" (NKJV). It took some time for me to realize that the Lord wanted to heal these wounds within me. Now I have this verse hung in a very visible place in my office. I want all of the wounded people who enter our counseling clinic to know this great information.

Because we are loved by God, we can then be merciful and loving to ourselves and subsequently to our spouse. It is with this insight that the tenets of soul healing love were formed.

Here they are.

The Five Basic Tenets of Soul Healing Love

1. God loves us unconditionally, and this love heals our soul wounds and restores us to wholeness.
2. This love helps us see ourselves through God's eyes, and learn to love ourselves as God does, imperfections and all.
3. Because we feel loved and lovable, we can allow God's grace and love to spill over onto our spouse. We can see our spouse through God's eyes and love him or her as God does.
4. Soul healing love brings about trust, vulnerability, and sharing that bonds us as a couple and merges us into a deep oneness.
5. This oneness replicates the oneness we feel with God; therefore, our love for our spouse and his or her love for us also restores us both to wholeness. Just as the love of God is soul healing, so the love between a husband and a wife is soul healing, as well.

This love is given to our mate out of appreciation and gratitude to God because of His love for us. It is in response to God's love that we love our partner. Soul healing love comes out of our fullness and our healthy self-esteem, not out of our lack.

God's Love for Us—Our Example

This soulful love of ourselves, as God loves us, gives us the energy to merge with the soul of another without the fear that we will be controlled, suffocated, or abused. As we become familiar with our own wounds, personality quirks, flesh patterns, and human frailties, we also become familiar with those of our spouse. We learn to understand and even appreciate all of the aspects of both souls, the good and the evil, the light as well as the shadow.

Rather than entering into a lifetime commitment with what we can gain in the forefront of our minds, we enter with the notion that we are going to love our mates as God loves us. We also begin to allow God's unconditional love or *agape* to penetrate us and fill us with His love and presence. This enables us to see ourselves through His eyes, as His creation. The outgrowth of this is that we are now energized to love ourselves and our partners unconditionally.

Because God loves us, we can love another. Healing our past hurts, accepting those things we cannot change, and forgiving our perpetrators becomes a conscious and unconscious goal. As our soul's journey continues, it is fueled by a desire to share this love with others. This energy finds another soul, merges with it, and begins the process of knowing and being known by another. We learn to accept each other, baggage and all.

The pain of our past actually hurts our mate just as it once hurt us. Healing our mate's wounds also heals our own. We desire to love our mate and help them love themselves. We want to share God's unconditional love (*agape*) with our partner because we have so richly experienced it as one of God's very own, special children. First John 4:11 says, "Dear friends, since God so loved us, we also ought to love one another" (NIV). As both husbands and wives bask in God's love, they will strongly desire to share it with each other. It is from God's wonderful love for us that soul healing love is born.

Love Is Reciprocal

When you give soul healing love to your spouse, the energy of this union has a reciprocal effect. Because you are loved unconditionally, you will spontaneously desire to go beyond the usual self-serving rituals of love to a more transcendent *agape* for your mate. This sets up an endless cycle of giving and receiving. Selfishness is replaced with a spontaneous reciprocity of caring. You cannot outgive your mate, and vice versa.

Love Is Learning

As you begin the journey as a soul healing partner, you will learn a great deal about your past emotional hurt and pain (or your soul wounds), as well as learn what has wounded your partner. You will realize that much of this pain accounts for both of your coping styles and relationship struggles today. In fact, much of the pain you inflict upon each other in your marriage is a direct or indirect result of the pain you have experienced earlier in life.

Upon realizing the woundedness in both you and your spouse, you then move beyond the typical power struggles that couples have and learn to love each other as friends and lovers, warts and all. This is not merely a toleration of each other's warts and scars, but an empathy and understanding of your mate's soul that inspires a deep care. This love allows you to wait patiently and prayerfully for your spouse's spiritual, soulful transformation. You do not ignore the wounds your mate inflicts upon you in denial, but you do not react so powerfully to this wounding that you retaliate in a very unhealthy or "unhealing" manner.

In loving your mate with a soul healing love, you will strongly desire to hear about the wounds of his or her past. In return, your partner will patiently listen as you share painful stories of your childhood. Both of you will develop empathy that will allow you to experience your partner's pain as if it were your own.

Love Is Koinonia

The Greek word *koinonia* was used a great deal in the Jesus Movement of the 1960s and 1970s to describe Christian sharing. Many churches picked it up as a catch phrase for Bible studies and fellowship groups. The true meaning of the word actually applies here, however. The word *koinonia* is defined as mutual empathy. What it means is that when your husband or wife shares his or her pain with you, you feel it with them. You respond as if the same pain is also happening to you, as well. This *koinonia* merges both of your souls into one. When your partner's soul aches, your soul will bleed, and vice versa. His or her wounds become your own, and healing him or her will eventually heal you, as well.

Love Your Mate As You Love Yourself

Ephesians 5:28 commands husbands to "love their wives as their own bodies. He who loves his wife loves himself" (NIV). The Living Bible says that husbands should love their wives as a part of themselves: "For since a man and his wife are now one, a man is really doing himself a favor and loving himself when he loves his wife!" If we as couples would really heed this wisdom, it would truly transform marriages today.

God's Plan for Us

What a marvelous plan God intended. Two souls united with synergistic passion. The energy this creates brings healing. Because of this mutual sharing, you are really doing yourself a favor by loving your partner, and vice versa. By giving to your partner, you also receive. By listening to your partner's soul, yours is heard. When you tell your partner what you need and he or she gives it to you, the giving of this gift will not only heal you, but his or her soul will be healed as a result. This mutual reciprocity is God's glorious design for marriage. In leaving and cleaving and becoming one, couples are exemplifying the Great Omnipotent Soul Healer, Jesus Christ. First John 4:10 says, "This is love: not that we loved God, but that he loved us and sent his Son as an atoning sacrifice for our sins" (NIV).

God in His infinite wisdom designed a love between a husband and a wife that replicates His own sacrificial love for His children. By seeking to become a soul healer to yourself and your partner, lover, and friend, you can become Christlike to him or her. As you model Christ's loving essence to the wounded soul of your better half, you are giving them the greatest present anyone could ever bestow upon them. Only the Creator of the universe could design a marvelous reciprocity of sharing such as this.

The notion of such loving and caring between partners almost boggles the mind. As young children growing up in dysfunctional families, we never dreamed this kind of love was possible. Many of our clients share this skepticism about love, perhaps because they also were raised in similar homes. Here is a story of two fellow skeptics.

Jim and Karen's Story

Jim and Karen were one such skeptical couple. Jim swaggered into the counseling office and introduced himself with a hearty handshake. Karen, also alive and bubbly, followed, holding little eight-year-old Jimmy's hand. After the rest of the introductions were made, Karen began telling me why they came. It seems that little Jimmy was just about to be suspended from school because of his disruptive behavior. He was not applying himself in class, and was getting into fights on the playground. Since Jimmy went to a small private school, these kinds of behavior problems were not tolerated. The principal had given Jimmy and his family one last chance before expelling him, and sent them to our counseling office.

It is typical for us in our clinic to complete a family history of both parents in the first session. So I (Bev) began my investigation. "Are your parents still living, Jim? Is there any history of alcoholism in either your parents or grandparents?"

"What?" Jim exclaimed. "I thought we were here to talk about my son! Why are you asking me all these questions about my parents? What do my parents have to do with Jimmy failing school?" he asked skeptically.

I began to explain to Jim: "They have everything to do with who *you* are as a person and who you have become as a parent, and therefore they have had a great direct and indirect effect on your son, Jimmy."

Jim gave Karen the cynical eye roll I have seen so often by parents in counseling. Karen looked at him as if to say, "Please give this a try," so Jim continued.

It did not take me long to put the pieces of this family's history together. Jim and Karen had both been raised in military families. Karen's father was an alcoholic who had begun drinking heavily when he retired. Karen was only eleven years old when this happened.

Jim admitted that his father drank heavily, but he couldn't say whether or not he was an alcoholic. Both of their mothers were described as compliant, passive women who were dominated by their husbands. This often happens in military homes. As you can see, Jim and Karen selected mates with complimentary or similar childhood wounds. This is a common occurrence though couples do not consciously seek this out. The attraction is unconscious.

I asked each person how they were disciplined when they were children. Once again I got the skeptical look from Jim. By this time Karen had a look of her own. She cut her eyes over to Jim with as much force as she could muster. Her look told Jim to leave his skepticism at the door. I was winning Karen over.

Karen began first, telling me that her father was critical and demanding. As she continued, her voice grew softer and her thoughts more pensive, as if she were seeing in her mind's eye what she had experienced as a child. This phenomenon often happens in counseling. The person looks back into their past and envisions childhood happenings. These happenings are complete with the emotions that were felt at that time.

It is not uncommon to see a grown person weeping like a child when he or she remembers the pain of their childhood. This occurrence has been given many names, from "flashbacks" to "retroflection." In the Soul Healing Love Model, we call these *regressive reflections*. Regressive reflections are extremely important in showing people how they deal with current family relationships. There is a saying that "those who forget the past are condemned to repeat it." This can also be true for those who painfully remember it.

As Karen began to regressively reflect on the experiences in her childhood, she wept quietly. Jim became very uncomfortable and began squirming in his seat. With her voice shaking, Karen painted a painful picture of her father's unhealthy dealings with his children. Karen, being the middle child of three girls, seemed to get more of her dad's wrath than her sisters did.

"So you see, Dr. Bev," she said, "This is why we came. I don't want Jim and I to repeat my parents' mistakes." Karen sucked back her tears with a little embarrassment, and looked appealingly at Jim.

Jim's discomfort was evident as we turned our attention to him.

"Now I know my dad drank," said Jim in a defensive tone, "but I don't believe he was as bad as Karen's dad. He did have high expectations of us and he was a perfectionist, but he just wanted the best for his children. Dad grew up poor, and he wanted us to have what he couldn't. As the oldest of two boys, I guess he expected more from me than my brother, and he was strict. But I can't remember him really, what you would call, abusing me."

"Don't you remember," Karen interrupted, "when he hit you right before he sent you to military school?" Karen looked at me and said, "Jim told me about this when we were dating. There were other instances, too, when I think Jim's dad was too harsh in disciplining him." Her misty-eyed look encouraged me to keep going. She looked as if she were saying nonverbally that I was on to something.

I did keep going, but I could tell that Jim was fearful. It was as if he had something to hide. He seemed to shut down and become determined not to show any emotion, like he was going to report just the facts, not feelings.

I then asked the two of them how they disciplined Jimmy. Jim began to look very uncomfortable at that point. Karen began again to weep softly. As she spoke, it became apparent that she was unhappy about how Jim had been treating Jimmy.

She felt that Jim was abusive to little Jimmy in an effort to get him to obey. She also said that she feared he had adopted some of his own father's extremely critical perfectionism in raising his children. Karen went on to say that *she* even felt unloved by Jim at times because he was hurting one of her most precious possessions, her son.

"If he loved us, he would not treat us this way! I even secretly doubt if I can stay in this marriage when Jim treats Jimmy like this," she said.

Jim looked shocked, but guilty. He realized that he was not only hurting his son with his impatient, abusive tendencies, but that he was also hurting his wife. He was concerned that his family had been so hurt by him, and that Karen felt that he was becoming like his father. The idea of his ever becoming that way sent cold chills down his spine. It was hard for him to see that he was doing some of the very things that he despised in his father. He had a great deal of guilt about this. This guilt worked to his and his family's advantage, however, because he made another appointment right away, and began to put his faith in Christian counseling and soul healing love to help them heal.

As the weeks went by, Jim and Karen revealed to each other many scenes of childhood pain. They learned how to comfort each other and lend support to each other's souls as they shared their pain. This bonded them in a way that they had not previously known. It wasn't easy, but they allowed God's love and forgiveness to heal the wounds that they had intentionally and unintentionally inflicted upon each other. They attended a Soul Healers Couples' Weekend with us, where we spend an entire weekend helping couples unpack childhood hurts, as well as see how these wounds were triggered in their adult relationships. There Jim and Karen learned communication tools and techniques, like the ones you will learn in this book, to help them resolve conflict, reconcile differences, and give and receive forgiveness. Through time, they became soul healing lovers to each other.

As for Jimmy, we were all amazed. When his mom and dad grew closer, he became much more peaceful and his behavior became more stable. We frequently see this in our office. When couples are not getting along, their children start having problems. The blessing is that when they become soul healers to each other, it begins to calm and heal their children, as well.

We spent some time in counseling teaching Mom and Dad more refined parenting tools, and teaching Jimmy the logical consequences of his actions. Jimmy was also tested, and we discovered that he had attention deficit disorder, which we began to treat through tutoring and medication. Upon further investigation, we discovered that Dad (Jim) also had attention deficit disorder. He learned that he had compensated for it all those years through overachievement and perfectionism. This awareness helped Jim to understand and better relate to his son.

It has been many years since this family committed themselves to becoming soul healers. We still bump into them periodically. Jim and Karen's relationship continues to flourish and is a blessing to our own souls. Jimmy is now doing quite well in school. He is 6'2" tall and weighs 220 pounds, and plays offensive and defensive tackle for his school's football team. In the stands sit his two greatest fans—Mom and Dad.

In order for this kind of soul transformation to take place, Jim and Karen had to begin to develop a clear understanding of the soul. Not only was this necessary for them, but we have found that it is also necessary for all those who wish to become soul healers. It is vitally important, then, to discern the purpose of the soul. The next chapter will actually give you a working definition of the soul.

CHAPTER 2

THE PURPOSE OF
THE SOUL

*W*hen we speak on soul healing love at retreats or workshops, we are often asked to define the soul. Many
people tell us that they think they know what the soul is but
they are not sure how to put it into words. Their questions
have caused us to study the soul from many different aspects
and to teach future soul healers what we have learned. Over
the years, we have realized that this is an awesome task, and
one that can only be completed with much reverence and respect.

Many philosophers, theologians, and psychologists have
discussed the soul. While we do not claim to have their abun-
dant knowledge, we do feel the need to develop a working
definition of the soul, so that you, the reader, can fully grasp
the depth of what we are trying to convey. The task that is set
before us is to stretch ourselves philosophically, with much humility, to define the word *soul* for our readers.

Most people say that the soul is the part of us that transcends life. Webster defines the soul as the principle of life. It is
that core energy or life energy that is both the invisible and
sentient elements of humans. It is the spiritual part of humans,
or one's moral aspect, believed to survive in the life hereafter,
which means that it is subject to happiness or misery in the life
to come. The soul is the true, real, emotional nature of a human
being. It is the substance or essence of who he or she is.[1]

Grolier's Encyclopedia defines the soul as the spiritual part of human beings that animates their physical existence and survives death. Grolier goes on to say that soul is a term rarely used with precise definition in philosophy, religion, or common life.[2] As we began to research a clear definition of the soul, we were inclined to agree.

In Scripture, the Greek word for soul is *psuche*. This is close to our English version of *psyche*, meaning breath, or breath of life. Since God made the soul as the central aspect of man that is most like Him, the soul is probably the most God-like part of the human psyche. The soul's God-like nature causes it to be capable of great depth and caring. It is this aspect of the soul that can merge with a partner and create the oneness discussed in Ephesians 5:31: "For this reason a man will leave his father and mother and be united to his wife, and the two will become one flesh" (NIV). Being aware of the capabilities of one's soul, as well as its frailties, can help couples achieve the oneness God has designed for them.

Vine's Bible Dictionary differentiates soul from spirit by clarifying that the spirit is man's higher nature, while the soul is man's lower element. Thus, things that are said to be sensed or felt in one's spirit may not necessarily be felt in the soul, as well. *Vine's* sees the soul as the day-in-and-day-out essence of life, the inhaling and exhaling of one's being.[3]

One aspect of defining and caring for the soul is what John and Paula Sanford call "the healing of memories." This term was made popular in Christian counseling circles during the last two decades. Their work discusses the transformation of the inner person, which is a soul cleansing, soul healing process that helps mend the soul from past abuses, in order to allow the soul to soar freely and grow spiritually.[4]

The Sanfords make the point that healing negative memories from one's past can prepare one's soul to worship God and to better love humankind. We see people every day in our counseling center who have little or no awareness of the hurt and pain that is in their souls. These people have a great deal of trouble in their relationships, and do not seem to understand why. Some of them are not Christians, so it is more understandable that they would be blind to aspects of the soul. But Christians can have a wealth of knowledge about their souls because the Creator of the universe inhabits them and wants to use them for His will and purpose. If this awareness is missing, inner healing may be necessary.

Thomas Moore, in his modern-day classic, *The Care of the Soul*, says, "Tradition teaches that soul lies midway between understanding and unconsciousness, and that instrument is neither the mind nor the body, but imagination.... Fulfilling work, rewarding relationships, personal power, and relief from symptoms are all gifts of the soul."[5] Moore implies such reverence and respect for the soul that he discusses it as if it has its own intelligence or sense of power, often referring to it simply as *soul*. While he quotes psychology as a secular science, he says that the care of the soul is a sacred art.[6]

The purpose of this book is not to develop the perfect definition of the soul. We will leave that to the theologians and modern-day mystics. We are merely trying to find a clear, working definition of the soul to help you, the reader, begin the incredible voyage on the sea of self-discovery and the discovery of your partner. We may never fully understand the complexities or the mysteries of the soul in this lifetime. We have both tried for some thirty years and are still perplexed by its intricacies and awed by its power. For the purpose of this book, we will, however, refer to the soul as:

> *a man or woman's essence, their true and basic nature, their life breath or life energy.*

Thus, the soul is what renders life and vitality to humans. The soul is our vivacity, our verve, our energy. It is the resulting life constituted in the individual, and the body is the material organism that is animated by it. In this book, the term *soul* will refer to:

> *the real, true self, which will include emotions, will, appetites, and memories.*

The Soul Is Vulnerable

Because the soul contains emotions, appetites, and memories, it is vulnerable to pain and hurt. Emotional hurts from the past can have a great impact on the soul. These hurts or soul wounds can offer a veritable wealth of knowledge about how a person relates to all aspects of life, as well as how he or she interacts in love relationships.

For couples to develop soul healing love for each other, they will have to explore areas of their own soul, as well as areas of their mate's soul. This is a very difficult task because many people do not want to face the ugly, dark parts of themselves. Seeing one's soul for what it really is, the good and the bad, is extremely hard. Perhaps it is even harder for Christians because they are taught by the church to be good and righteous. Holiness is their goal, and therefore they feel guilty when they see their sinful nature appear. It is this graceless guilt that causes a person not to face his or her sin and deal with it. Many people hide from the truth about themselves, and do not admit that their sin nature even exists. When they do stumble and sin, they quickly acknowledge their sin and then repress it, so that they never have a chance to truly confess it and learn about the unhealthy aspects of their souls in order to heal them.

To quote Thomas Moore, "Moralism is one of the most effective shields against the soul, protecting us from its intricacy."[7] If we are too moralistic or judgmental about our own soul, we will be equally judgmental, if not more so, about the soul of our spouse. Getting to know our own soul and loving it as God does will help us to give as well as receive love in our relationships.

The Soul and Fear

What happens when one wounded soul sails aimlessly upon the sea of relationships and comes in contact with the repressed wounded soul of another? The books, songs, and movies speak to us of romantic bliss, happily ever after—two lost souls now joyfully found, never to suffer again! This is not what statistics show us. "Happily ever after" keeps getting shorter all the time.

Not only are we seeing more marriages break up these days, but we are also seeing more commitment phobia in singles. We wrote about this in our book, *The Singlehood Phenomenon: Ten Brutally Honest Reasons Singles Are Not Getting Married* (2006). In our research, we discovered that these young urbanites are skeptical about marriage so they are choosing alternatives like cohabitation and non-married co-parenting instead. If they do marry, they are waiting longer before they tie the knot. This may be good, in that these singles are being more selective in the matrimonial process, but with the high divorce rate, coupled with the lower pleasure index of married couples, perhaps fear is really more of the culprit here.

These young would-be partners see marriage as a jail sentence rather than a life-enhancing commitment. They are afraid that marriage will take away their quality of life. Rather than take that chance, they remain single. There are those, however, who take their chances with marriage, and in ignorance become frightened with their choice.

Commitment Equals Chaos

Commitment has a way of causing paranoia in many souls. Harville Hendrix, in his book *Getting the Love You Want*, says that committed love brings out the archaic fear of death in people. Lovers move to a very infantile place in their unconscious as they try to learn to trust each other[8]. Because of this, couples usually have a major conflict within seventy-two hours after making a commitment. Many times, this is because their ability to trust has been fractured. People who grew up in homes where their caregivers were not reliable can have problems with trust. Perhaps their parent or parents were alcoholics or worked all the time. Maybe their father or mother was away for a long period of time. These situations can wreak havoc on a person's ability to build trust in relationships.

Since the basis of a romantic relationship requires the soul to trust, these people are consciously or unconsciously fearful of making this kind of commitment. Falling in love reminds them of their primary love relationship (that of their parents), and this scares them to death. They have difficulty giving their partners all the privileges of their love, because with those privileges come all the power to be hurt, as well. These wounded souls are all too aware that if they fall in love, their partner then has a great deal of power over them, and this is scary. One could say that these people have "broken trusters."

Basic Trust

Those of you who took Psychology 101 will remember Harry Harlow's study of monkeys. Harlow had two groups of baby monkeys. Both groups were given surrogate mothers. One of the surrogate mother monkeys was made of cloth, and while she could give her babies warmth, she could not feed them. The other mother monkey was made of wire. She was, however, rigged to be able to nurse the baby monkeys. Harlow found that, even though the baby monkeys could not get food from the warm cloth mother, they still preferred her over the cold wire surrogate. As the study showed, many of the monkeys failed to thrive under the care of the wire monkey.

I will never forget the picture in my psychology book of two baby monkeys clinging to each other tightly, filled with such fear and insecurity. Harlow dubbed these monkeys "together-together monkeys." The outcome of his study showed that monkeys (as well as humans) need warmth and security, not just food, in order to learn what he called "basic trust." Without "basic trust," insecurity grows, and all further relationships will suffer.[9]

Many of us go into relationships like those clinging baby monkeys who have shattered "trusters." I (Bev) have often said that I was raised by a "wire mother" who, because of her own soul wounds, was not capable of loving me. Many of the people we see in counseling share similar feelings about their parents. With this kind of upbringing, we enter into committed relationships somewhat handicapped. What we want with all of our hearts is to love and be loved, yet this causes us so much angst that we have a hard time embracing it. Getting the love we so desperately want scares us to death. It arouses all of our suspicions and anxieties. It is both desired and feared. Our anxiety levels are high because unconditional love is so unfamiliar to us.

Wish Fulfillment Theory

Sigmund Freud wrote of what he called the "wish fulfillment theory," in which he postulated that with the fulfillment of every wish comes the fear that it will not be granted again. Thus, getting what you wish for causes anxiety. This is especially true when it comes to romantic love because it is our deepest and most basic soul need. The fear of that love being taken away after it has been given is equal to the fear of death. People literally fear the destruction of their own soul at the hands of their partner. Knowing this truth, it is easy to see not only how people can fear love, but also become obsessed with the loved one. Stalking, revenge, suicide threats, and other types of unhealthy behavior are a result of this sort of addictive love. These people have identified their former partner with the very survival of their soul.

With such high expectations placed on love, one can see how marriage can become a formula for chaos. Many people yield to their anxiety and exit the marriage, only to find themselves repeating the same unhealthy patterns, or continuing to be at risk for further aimless searching on the sea of relationships. These lovers search for the "right one" instead of looking inward to their own souls for the answer. Often times the "right one" is directly in front of them, but a lack of awareness of the soul blinds them from its realization.

As you can see, discovering the purpose of the soul and understanding the soul's attributes can help individuals learn how to merge into the mysterious oneness that God has intended for His children. Lack of awareness and understanding can thwart this merger. The following is a story of a Christian couple who came into counseling having very little awareness of what their soul was all about.

Greg and Marsha's Soul Exploration

Marsha was a very pleasant, overweight woman who came to our counseling center because she was not able to control her eating. Food had become a compulsion for her. During her first session, she said that she had waited a long time to decide to seek help because Greg, her husband, did not believe in counseling. Whenever she would share her struggles over food with him, he would accuse her of not praying enough for self-control, or suggest that she do more Bible study.

While this hurt Marsha, she was inclined to agree with him. She would then feel bad and try even harder to control her eating. Greg finally agreed that she could go to counseling, and that he would accompany her a few times. However, he made it very clear that he was not coming in for himself. He wanted us to be clear that it was Marsha who had the problem, not him.

Similar Wounds

As I was exploring their family histories, I discovered that both Greg and Marsha had very similar childhood soul wounds. Each had actually selected a partner who was wounded in the same way. They also had some of the same issues to deal with in their families of origin. They were both the oldest child in their families. Marsha had two younger brothers, and Greg had a younger brother and a younger sister. Both described their parents as strict and controlling. Both rebelled as teens, skipped school, made bad grades, and got involved in the drug culture. It is amazing how many times couples come in and tell us that their pasts were alike in key ways.

Bev and I were no exception. We, too, discovered that we were wounded at the same stages of life. When she was thirteen years old, she found out that her brother was using drugs and this was a very painful time for her. When I was thirteen, I discovered that my dad was cheating on my mom. This was equally painful. While we dated, we shared many painful stories from our childhood with each other and felt very much at home and accepted by one another. It is not that we were conscious that these similarities were drawing us together. We were not that smart or aware at that time. It was just that unconsciously we felt right at home with each other. We now know that this was in some ways because of these parallel issues in our past. Harville Hendrix in his great book, *Keeping the Love You Find*, calls this "the phenomenon of recognition.[10]"

This phenomenon of recognition is what makes you feel like you have known your partner all of your life. It causes you to read each other's minds and finish each other's sentences. This can be attributed to the fact that you unconsciously seek people who have been through similar situations in childhood, like Bev and I did.

Of course, when we dated, we did not consciously ask if our childhood soul wounds were similar and how. It was not until we started developing the Soul Healing Love Model that we realized just how similar they were. People do not typically interview prospective partners and rule out those people who do not have similar wounds. They, like us, simply feel more at home and comfortable with these people. They feel the phenomenon of recognition like Greg and Marsha did.

After they were married, Greg and Marsha continued to live life in the "fast lane," drinking very heavily and using drugs regularly. Marsha quit drinking when she got pregnant, but Greg continued to drink and take drugs. Following the birth of their first child, they decided to rededicate their lives to Christ. They began to go to church and immediately became involved there. The transformation for Greg was tremendous. He gave up drugs and alcohol. With tears in his eyes, he shared about how he never wanted to use drugs or drink after that time. Several weeks after his conversion, he also gave up cigarettes and said that he never had the desire to smoke again. Greg gave God the credit for the change that took place in his life. He felt like his soul was where it needed to be. He was going to church and living a godly life. What more could he ask for?

Whenever someone would ask Greg how he gave up such addictive habits, he would, in preacher-like style, tell them, "I just did it!" Now, while that advice would be good for a Nike advertisement ("Just Do It"), it was not so good for simple church folks who struggled with compulsive behaviors. It was especially damaging to his wife, who had tried hard to control her eating, but had a very difficult time doing so.

After a while, Marsha began to feel unloved by Greg. His judgmental, shaming style was taking its toll on their marriage. When I asked Greg about this, his response was typical of his preacher-like attitude: "Marsha, like most people, just doesn't want to hear the truth about her sin. She wants me to feel sorry for her and make excuses for her. Well, I can't pity someone who just needs to get a grip on herself and practice some of the fruit of the Spirit, like self-control. Marsha wants her 'ears tickled' [to hear what she wants to hear]." This type of response would send Marsha into a tailspin, and she would feel hopeless and depressed—and eat even more.

Marsha told Greg many times that she felt unloved by him. Greg would call these statements "ridiculous nonsense," and quote scriptures to her about God's command to him to love his wife, and his determination to obey, no matter what the price. Needless to say, this did not help Marsha feel more loved and cherished by him.

He, in turn, felt that Marsha did not care about him. This was because he had told her many times that her weight was a problem to him, but he felt that she would not lose weight just to spite him. This created a great deal of conflict, especially in their sex life. Marsha struggled with her negative body image and her negative feelings for Greg. The result was that she had no sexual desire. Greg, on the other hand, lost his sexual desire because he wanted an attractive, shapely spouse who took care of herself. I could quickly see how her issues and his issues were working against each other.

Opposite Adaptations

Not only do couples find partners with similar wounds, but often they have opposite adaptations to those wounds. Marsha dealt with her teen rebellion by connecting to her peer group and fellow rebels. Greg was a loner. He did drugs and drank alone most of the time, with the exception of using with Marsha. Marsha tended to deal with life's stresses by connecting to other people. She would typically pick weaker friends whom she could join with and take care of. She admitted that she went for the underdog and tried to get people to be more understanding of their plight. This is exactly what she did with Greg. She often played the role of caretaker with him as a teen, and took his side over his "judgmental, harsh parents."

Why, you may ask, is this important information, and what does it have to do with their marriage now? The answer is—a lot! Marsha's adaptation to life is to join, pursue, and caretake. Greg's is to distance, be a loner, and pull away from people. These are opposite adaptations to the same wound. We see in this example, as in many areas of dating and mating, that opposites attract. The caretaker finds the loner. The pursuer finds the isolator, and the clinger finds the avoider.

During courtship, couples seem to love these opposite adaptations. They often say they feel "whole and fulfilled" with each other. Being in the presence of their opposite often makes them feel more complete. But when the honeymoon is over and the conflicts start, couples find that these differences are the very things they fight about. This was true of Greg and Marsha.

Marsha dealt with her struggles with food by joining diet clubs and Bible studies. Greg would tell her to stop talking and start dieting. His harsh, distant approach offended Marsha, and her lingering issue with weight offended Greg. You see from their conflict that their adaptations to their soul wounds were actually very wounding to each other.

The main thing that Marsha needed from Greg—understanding, empathy, and connection—was what Greg struggled to give. The major thing that Greg needed from Marsha—the strength to stand alone and change her unhealthy eating habits—was what Marsha had trouble doing. By the time Greg and Marsha came to our counseling office, they were almost convinced that they had married the wrong person because their wounds were impacting each other in such a negative way. The truth is that they did indeed pick the *right* person, because their wounds impacted each other in a negative way.

You see, the only way that Greg could heal Marsha was to move to a place of mercy and grace with regard to her eating struggles. This would cause him to have to face his unhealthy adaptations to his childhood wounds and allow the Lord to bring healing to him. The Lord had to help this loner become a joiner. If he did this, he would not only heal his struggling wife, but he, in turn, would be healed of his unhealthy distancing pattern. Conversely, Marsha would have to stop her unhealthy clinging patterns and allow the Lord to give her the strength to stand alone against her compulsive eating. So you see, in making a move to heal each other, the Lord could paradoxically heal them. The truth is that the best person to heal Marsha was Greg, because he was her opposite, and the best person to heal

Greg was Marsha for the same reason. The problem was that neither knew enough about their own souls and the soul wounds hidden there to start this healing process.

It was apparent to us that both Greg and Marsha had a very limited idea of the soul. They were both ignoring previous soul wounds, which they had repressed or covered up by using drugs and alcohol. This repression caused them to act out in unhealthy ways. They were not only abusing their own souls, but they were also abusing each other's. Both thought that finding salvation was all that they needed. To quote Marsha, "I thought that once I became a Christian that was all I needed to do to live a good life." Many new Christians, like Marsha, feel that this is the final act for the soul. However, it is really just the beginning. God wants to use His awesome power to continue to heal the wounds of our souls, and also to heal the woundedness of our partners as they in turn heal us.

As for Greg and Marsha, they began to learn about each other's souls. They shared experiences and feelings with each other that they had not shared before. Greg learned that Marsha had been sexually assaulted as a young girl. He sat lovingly and patiently as she shared how painful this was for her, and how it still affected her sexual attitudes and body image to that day. Marsha learned that Greg's father never showed love for him physically or verbally. Marsha listened as he shared how he felt that he had to earn God's love by performing, just as he had had to earn his own father's approval. In their sharing, they opened each other's eyes to the pain in their souls.

Greg developed empathy and understanding for Marsha, which helped him not to be so judgmental. As Greg became less judgmental and acted in a more loving manner to Marsha, Marsha wanted to reach out to him and please him. She wanted to be thin, which would not only please Greg, but would also (she discovered) heal herself. So, by learning about their souls, these two brave sojourners learned to develop a soul healing love for one another.

Now, years later, Marsha describes Greg as her best friend and her biggest advocate. She still has to maintain discipline about her desire for food, but she feels free from the pain that this compulsive behavior caused her. Greg runs a street ministry to help homeless people find Christ and get back on their feet. He regularly says that he could not be ministering with the compassion and empathy that he has today, had it not been for all he learned from his soul healing journey.

Greg and Marsha were excellent examples of healing to each other. There were things they learned from each other that they could learn from no other person. In counseling they learned that souls are sacred and should be loved and cherished. They gained a new, healthy respect for the soul. The interactive nature of the wounds they had inflicted upon each other were transformed into healing balm for their soul's pain.

In order for us to heal our souls and to prepare our souls to heal others, we must first examine the environment in which they were formed. Getting in touch with what has happened to us, or finding out what wounded us, will help heal our souls. Facing our past hurts and wounds also helps us learn to see the wounds of others. Mutual sharing of soul pain can then become a part of our relationships. The next chapter will be dedicated to the arduous, yet rewarding, task of examining the environment of the soul.

CHAPTER 3

THE SOUL IN PAIN

I asked God for strength that I might achieve,
   I was made weak that I might learn to humbly obey.
I asked God for health that I might do greater things,
   I was given infirmity that I might do better things.
I asked God for power that I might have the praise of men,
   I was given weakness that I might feel the need for God.
I asked for all things that I might enjoy life,
   I was given life that I might enjoy all things.
I got nothing that I asked for, but everything that I hoped for,
   Almost despite myself, my unspoken prayers were answered.
I am, among all, most richly blessed!
           Author Unknown

*C*arol, an attractive, middle-aged woman, came into our counseling office because her marriage was in trouble. She had been married to Mike for twenty-eight years, and she said that over time they had grown apart. Mike generally traveled all week, and spent the majority of his weekends on the golf course. Since the youngest of their three daughters had gone off to college, Carol had become very lonely. She began to actively seek out Mike's company, but when she did, she found him to be detached, grumpy, and emotionally unavailable. When she would try to engage him in a conversation, he would get angry and close up even tighter. She was at the end of her rope and said that if things did not change, she was moving out.

Carol had sensed that Mike had started drifting away from her about ten years earlier, but, like many wives, she ignored that which was too painful to deal with, and threw herself into raising her children. Now that the kids were grown, Carol had to do some serious soul searching. What had happened to her relationship with Mike? Had they both drifted away? Could they recover their passion and love for each other? Did each really want to? In answering these questions, Carol soon came upon some painful realizations.

When she confronted Mike with her concerns, he blew up, blaming her for being critical. Carol felt hopeless and despondent and begged him to come to therapy, but he would have no part of it. She finally talked him into attending one of our Soul Healers Couples' Workshops. Reluctantly, Mike came and sat there listening to the theories about how the soul wounds from childhood can affect one's marital relationship.

During the weekend, Mike was squirming in his chair, and it was obvious that he was uncomfortable with the topic. Finally, he could not take it anymore and so he spoke up and asked, "How could something that happened forty years ago that I cannot even remember have anything to do with my marriage to Carol today?"

It was hard to believe, with all the material written about self-help and inner healing, and all the television talk shows in the last two decades, that Mike had no awareness of this kind of pain. But he didn't—or rather, wouldn't—entertain the idea that soul wounds even existed. In the Soul Healing Love Model, we define a *soul wound* as a need from childhood that was not met. The reason we look specifically at childhood is that most self-development is completed in a child by age seven. These early years of life play a key part in forming the psyche. Traumatic events that happened during these years can affect people long into their adult years if they are not dealt with. While it is true that people can have soul wounds in adulthood, childhood wounds can often be the most problematic.

Perhaps one of the most difficult aspects of the Soul Healing Love Model is getting people to look at the soul wounds that occurred in their family of origin. People often have a hard time looking at their parents as wounders in any way because they feel guilty doing so. The trouble is that our parents are very powerful figures in our early development. For the infant, they hold in their power the child's very survival. They can make the whole world light or dark simply by the flip of a switch. Infants and children are not sophisticated enough to know that parents are mere mortals, thus to them, they hold the power of the universe in their hands. If they intentionally or unintentionally misuse this power, children can pay for this pain as adults. People may also not want to look at their childhood soul wounds because they do not want to face the pain that goes with it.

We gently, yet determinedly, helped Mike begin to open up to an awareness of his childhood issues. We suggested that he had probably repressed a good portion of his early memories because they were too painful to remember.

"Does everything in my marriage have to be about a wound? What if it really is my wife who is causing the problem and I don't have any soul wounds to speak of?" was his frustrated query.

"No, everything does not have to be about a soul wound," we responded. "It is not that your mate is not guilty in some way. She indeed needs to take responsibility for what she has done. We are simply saying that your extreme reaction might indicate that a soul wound from childhood is being triggered and needs attending. These wounds can tell you a lot about yourself and why you feel the way you feel and react the way you do."

After much resistance, Mike again asked a question, only this time he was much softer. "Why?" he asked pleadingly. "Why should I go back there and look at the painful things that happened in my past? Shouldn't they just stay buried?" We have to give this answer to wounded people all the time. All we said was, "Because, Mike, the Lord wants you to remember your pain so He can heal it."

We have a saying in the Soul Healing Love Model that we borrowed from Alcoholics Anonymous: "You can't heal what you can't feel." In order for Mike to heal his soul wounds, he would have to go through the door of pain. The good news is that he would have the Lord holding his hand and bringing him healing every step of the way.

Slowly but surely, Mike began to deal with these issues. He poured out stories about his prostitute mother and a father he never knew. His mother was very aloof and distant, and Mike did not feel wanted by her. When he was six years old, his mother was sent to prison, and he was placed in the home of his elderly paternal grandparents. Several years later, his grandmother passed away, leaving him with a cold and critical grandfather whom he said he could never please. At age sixteen, he left home and joined the military. He had been in some type of military service ever since.

Mike reached the rank of colonel and now served in the Army Reserves. He felt that the military gave him the structure and sense of belonging that he had never had in his life. In the military he was important and significant; in the military he was part of a "family," no longer an orphan who did not belong. This met a very deep emotional need for Mike, but the negative aspect was that he could relate to other people *only* as a colonel. He related to his wife and children in a harsh, military fashion.

Carol was raised in a Christian home, and said that her parents loved her, but always compared her to her beautiful and talented older sister. This made Carol feel that she was not good enough, so she tried hard to win people's approval. When Mike would relate to her in a severe fashion, this impacted her childhood inadequacy wound. Carol would then criticize Mike for his harshness, which would in turn remind him of his critical, aloof grandfather. Carol dealt with her soul wounds by trying to connect and talk things out. Unfortunately, most of her talking had become critical and negative. Mike dealt with this by withdrawing. It seemed that the more she tried to get him to talk, the more he withdrew. Once again, we see the principle of similar wounds but opposite adaptations playing out.

Being a husband and father was very difficult for Mike because he had had so little modeling of how a family was supposed to interact, let alone really love each other. His family- of-origin experience left him sorely lacking in relationship skills. Much of his childhood pain was locked in his unconscious mind, and he was not aware of it.

The Unconscious Mind

Dr. Larry Crabb, in his book, *Inside Out*, gives a great illustration of the typical human's awareness of the unconscious mind. Take a blank sheet of notebook paper and place a small dot in the center of the page. The small dot represents what we know about the unconscious mind, and the great white sea around it represents all that we do not know. In other words, the vast majority of our experiences, feelings, sensations, and reactions are acted out in relationships without our conscious awareness. This means that many of our motivations and actions in relationships are not known to us consciously. When we have no clue why we react the way we do in certain situations, the answer may be buried deep in our unconscious.[1]

For many people, like Mike, the notion of exploring the vast unknown regions of our unconscious can be frightening. Any known conscious memories of painful experiences can even deepen our reluctance to start digging through our psyches. Many of us resist looking at previous hurts. I (Bev) could empathize with him. It is painful to look at childhood wounds. I remember having to face my own painful past, some thirty years earlier.

Fear of Past Pain

As a graduate student, I had looked forward with anticipation to earning my degree in family therapy and then, of course, saving all of humankind. I had decided that I was going to single-handedly heal the brokenhearted and truly set the captives free. (If this sounds a bit Messianic, it's because it was.) One day in class, I was asked, much to my surprise, to share some of my own painful childhood memories with the other interns in the graduate program.

"What?" I cried, *"Me, relive my childhood? Are you kidding?"* I was terrified. *"It is done... gone... finished! I dealt with that stuff a long time ago! I've forgiven my parents for their benign neglect and their blatant abuse! I'm done with all of that!"*

I will never forget what my very wise graduate professor said then: "You may be finished with the pain, my dear—but the pain is not finished with you." She was right, of course. While I had repressed all the pain of a childhood filled with emotional, psychological, and physical violence, my soul had unconsciously adapted to its wounds by compulsively wanting to heal the pain in everyone else. What I did not realize was that my desire to be a soul healer could indeed only happen as I learned to allow God to heal my own soul.

The Door of Pain—A Door of Hope

I decided to give Mike and Carol the same opportunity that I was given those many years earlier—the chance to heal their souls. This healing journey begins with walking through the door of our unconscious minds and feeling the pain we dread to feel. I knew Mike and Carol would hate doing this, just as I had many years previously. Pain's haunting presence would creep into the dark recesses of my soul as if to suffocate me. But I knew that I had had to face my dreaded nemesis head-on.

So, as I had done, I guided Mike and Carol into the dark abyss of their soul's pain. They both began to discover something surprising about their journey. They actually saw that pain could be a friend, a positive teaching tool, a wise mentor that illuminated the soul. They learned that pain was not the real culprit. It was the inability to deal with pain that was the problem.

We are given pain as a signal to our psyches, as well as our bodies, of danger and possible injury. Pain tells us that we need attention. When we cut our finger, it hurts. The pain is a signal that we need to move in a healing direction. When we apply ointment and a bandage, we are then on the road to recovery. If our body had not reacted to the pain, we could not move toward healing.

The Gift of Pain

Dr. Paul Brand, a physician who worked for many years with lepers, thinks that the greatest problem in treating leprosy is that the afflicted persons have lost their ability to sense and feel pain. Because of this, their tissue can actually deteriorate long before any pain signal is sent to the brain. Lepers are then in serious physical trouble before they are even aware of it. Without feeling the pain, they cannot effectively deal with their disease. For a leper, pain is truly a gift.[2]

As soul healers, we, too, can learn to see pain as a gift. It can actually be viewed as the soul's signal fire, showing us where we need attention and healing. Pain, then, is not our problem, but rather a part of the solution, and therefore can become one of our greatest allies.

Society Views Pain Negatively

Feeling our pain can be very foreign in today's modern culture. Our western civilization has an aversion to dealing with pain and struggle. It is difficult for many people to see the value of grieving, or feeling the losses of the past. We are a generation of instant gratification, fast relief, and microwaved joy. If it hurts, numb it. If it aches, stop it. If it's broken, throw it out. And yet it is amazing that for a culture that spends billions of dollars annually on pain relief and need-gratification, we have so little pleasure to show for it.

Some Christians even have a negative slant on reliving their past hurt and pain, believing it is a sign of unforgiveness, or a holding on to the old sinful nature that is within them. Our view is to the contrary. We have seen that if people are willing to look at their past hurt, they can allow God's grace to heal it, and then put it behind them.

Leading people into their journey through pain has brought us to the conclusion that pleasure is not the absence of pain, nor is it pain's antonym. Rather, pain is actually a part of pleasure's process, a crucible, if you will, that not only signals that there is a need in the soul, but also helps the soul to bloom.

Feeling Is Healing

If we do not feel, then we cannot heal. Defense mechanisms may help for a while, but eventually our bodies and our souls will remind us of our repressed pain, in a way repaying us for not feeling it the first time. I (Bev), like many people we see, tried to deny that my past could haunt me. I even tried to deny that I had soul wounds. Many of our clients do this, especially those people who have suffered more passive abuse.

Often people who had relatively good childhoods resist looking at their past in order to protect their parents. It is not uncommon to have someone in our workshops or in our counseling office ask the somewhat unbelievable question, "What if I don't have any soul wounds?"

There is no such thing, we tell them. Everyone has been through some hard times. Some situations may not be as bad as others, but everyone has had some struggle to deal with. Often we tell them that if they believe that they are the only one in the world who has never had a soul wound, then we would like to bronze them, put them in our suitcase, and take them with us all across the globe to show as a specimen, because they would be the only person ever born to have survived life without being wounded.

Let's face it; if you went through junior high school in western civilization, you were wounded in some way. Most of us would never want to go through that time in our lives again because it was so difficult. Soul wounds are normal. They can occur because our parents, friends, family, or culture committed sins of commission or omission, or simply because they did not know any better.

Either way, frequently a person's first response to the idea of soul wounds is to resist feeling the pain that they caused. Like many other adult children of abuse, I (Bev) tried all kinds of ways to defend against feeling my childhood pain. I made excuses for my parents. I saw the "silver lining" in the dark clouds. I got busy trying to heal others. I read books about healing the dysfunctional family. I went to classes and attended seminars on inner healing. I did everything but *feel* the pain. All the while, my body kept score with depression, headaches, stomach problems, and fatigue.

I was not alone in my ignorance; many people's physical illnesses treated today have their roots in unresolved soul pain. These are called psychosomatic disorders. Even though so many people suffer from these types of maladies, most of them, like me, would rather wrestle a shark, or even take their chances with Daniel in the lion's den, than feel all the pain of the past. Yet it is the only way to truly be healed.

Mike and Carol's Journey through Pain

This was the journey we encouraged Mike and Carol, and many other folks, to take. Mike in particular had a hard time wondering why God had allowed so many painful things to happen to him as a child. The answer was found in the school of pain. Often when we walk with people back into their painful childhoods, we give them a scripture passage that has been very meaningful for us. This was also helpful for Mike and Carol. Romans 5:3–4 says, "We can rejoice, too, when we run into problems and trials, for we know that they are good for us— they help us learn to be patient. And patience develops strength of character in us and helps us trust God more each time we use it until finally our hope and faith are strong and steady" (TLB). With pain as their mentor, Mike and Carol began a healing journey, knowing that the things that had happened to them could help develop their hope and faith. That journey began with their families of origin.

Family of Origin

Family of origin is the therapeutic term for the family in which we were raised. This terminology is used in contrast to the term *nuclear family*, which is the family with whom we now live. To be more specific, our family of origin includes our parents, grandparents, and siblings, while our nuclear family includes us, our spouse, and our children.

Our family of origin provides us with much information about our childhood wounds. Our past tells us about who we are and why we do what we do in relationships. Most of our interactions with people were learned in our families of origin. For example, if we grew up in an emotionally abusive home, we may have a tendency to abuse or to be emotionally abused in our present relationships. Dr. Patricia Love, a well-known marital therapist and author, makes a startling statement in her seminars that "to the extent we have been abused in childhood, we can be abused or abuse."[3] Patterns of dysfunction may continue, unless we are willing to become aware of their effects.

Types of Soul Wounds

Dr. David Seamands, in his book *Healing Damaged Emotions*, writes about the types of families that may cause people pain throughout their lives. Homes where there was active alcoholism, violence, divorce, or the death of a parent or sibling can cause soul wounds.[4]

We qualify soul wounds into two categories: active and passive. Active wounds connote overt physical, verbal, and sexual abuse. Some examples of this may be beating, hitting, slapping, name calling, threatening, blaming, and shaming. My (Bev's) mother often made the statement that if abortion were legal, she would have gotten rid of me. This overt verbal abuse created a deep scar on my soul that stayed with me even as an adult. Examples of active sexual abuse are fondling, molestation, and intercourse, initiated by a parent or adult toward a child.

Passive wounds are more subtle or covert. This type of pain is more in the emotional or psychological area. Examples of this include emotional or physical neglect, not being told you were loved, not being hugged or physically nurtured, or being criticized for not being good enough. My (Tom's) dad was an expert at making me feel not good enough. He could do so by a simple look or gesture.

My father was forever doing projects around our house. As the only boy, I was his natural helper. The problem was that my dad was a very good doer and a very poor teacher. He would show me how to do something once, and when I could not get it, he would grab the tool out of my hand and say, "Just give me that. I'll do it." Now, he never told me that I was inferior or inadequate, but his actions, tone, and posture spoke volumes. The word that I internalized most around my dad was *idiot*. When I could not do what he tried to teach me, I internalized that I was simply an idiot. All he had to do was look at me a certain way and I knew I was an idiot.

The trouble with a wound is that not only do you *internalize* it, but you also *generalize* it, which means that if you believe it is true about yourself, then you believe it is true about everyone else out there.

As I grew up I made an amazing discovery: There are idiots out there everywhere, especially in traffic! It seemed that every time I got on the road and was in a hurry, there were idiots out there who would get in front of me and slow me down. I started to believe that there was a conspiracy of idiots that set out on the road just as I left my house. This often happened when I took our little girls to school on the way into the church where I worked as a pastor.

One day Bev took the girls to school because I had an early meeting. Thank goodness she drives sanely and stays well beneath the speed limit. She returned from dropping off the girls and reported what Mandy, our precocious five year old had said: "Mommy, where are all the idiots out there today?" "What?" Bev asked. "Yes, Mommy, Daddy saw seven of them on the way to school yesterday." We both got a big laugh out of this as I'm sure you do. But then I began to take stock of what I was teaching my daughter. If I thought that I was an idiot, and that everyone else out there were idiots, then she might worry that she had to do things correctly all the time so that she, too, would not be an idiot.

Mandy was our little perfectionist, and it was no wonder that I had to encourage her to stop erasing on her kindergarten papers so that they would be perfect, and quit scolding herself because she could not read everything that she picked up. She pushed herself very hard, and that day I learned where much of this came from. It came from the wounds that her granddad had inflicted upon her dad, and I had been unaware that I was passing down the same woundedness to her. She and I had many talks about how capable she was, and I'm glad to say that we stopped this curse at this generation. It amazed us how something so simple could provide such a profound lesson for us. Passive abuse can be subtle but potent nonetheless. It can also take on many forms.

Many people grew up with a father who worked long hours and spent a great deal of time away from home. Because of this, their children may carry a deep feeling of neglect or abandonment. If you grew up with a perfectionist mother who was constantly critical, you could be a victim of passive emotional abuse. If you grew up in a home with parents who did not love each other or who were in constant conflict, you may carry psychological or emotional scars from this. Overprotection and overindulgence are also two forms of passive abuse. Spoiled children can become narcissistic adults who feel entitled and who have unhealthy expectations in their adult relationships.

Examples of passive sexual abuse include being watched as you undress or bathe, inappropriate displays of parental nudity, obscene statements or gestures made by family members, or being made to look at indecent sexual material. Emotional incest is also a form of passive sexual abuse. This is where one parent puts all of their love and energy into their child rather than their mate. While there is no active sexual abuse, the child is made to play the role of the husband or wife in the family. This creates a very unhealthy enmeshment between parent and child. The child grows up feeling that love is suffocating, confining, and demanding.

Boys who were the victims of emotional incest by their mothers may have poor or estranged relationships with their fathers. Their unhealthy bonding with Mom not only makes Dad feel left out, but it also sets up an unhealthy sense of competition between father and son for Mom's affection and attention. Many men who have experienced such emotional incest fear connection and have adversarial, distant relationships with their wives.[5]

Detailed examples of both types of soul wounds are listed below.

Active Wounds
- **Physical**—hitting, slapping, beating
- **Verbal**—name calling, threatening
- **Emotional**—using fear and violence as a motivator
- **Sexual**—fondling, molestation, intercourse
  Passive Wounds
- **Physical**—being neglected or abandoned, left alone too often
- **Verbal**—being told you were not wanted or loved
- **Emotional**—overprotection, spoiling, emotional incest, being told that you were bad, being falsely blamed or shamed
- **Sexual**—demeaning sexual slurs, being leered at while undressing or bathing

All of these abuses can leave scars in a person's psyche. They can also be the seedbed in which relational trouble grows. Many of the adults we treat in our counseling center can trace their marital trouble back to childhood. If you are unsure whether you suffered from active or passive abuse, here are some symptoms that are characteristic of these people:

- Super-sensitivity
- Perfectionism
- Low self-esteem
- Sense of unworthiness
- Wrong idea of God
- Fear of failure
- Depression
- Fear of commitment
- Fear of rejection
- Lack of trust in self and others
- Active addictions, both negative and positive
- Lack of forgiveness
- Critical spirit
- Bitterness and resentment

While it is true that many of these characteristics can come naturally as part of our human nature or as a result of innate temperament, if you are having trouble in these areas, it is worth exploring your childhood to see if any roots exist.

It is often hard to look at our parents as perpetrators. Even if we grew up in blatantly dysfunctional homes where there was violence, alcoholism, incest, or mental illness, there is still a tendency to deny that our parents had any fault. We want to preserve their sacred image and believe that we experienced a "Leave-It-to-Beaver" family environment. In some ways this makes us feel like we are alright, as well.

Ivan Boze-Meninage, a famous French family therapist, once said, "Your parents are still your parents, whether they are a thousand miles away, or dead and buried. They have placed an indelible mark on your souls that transcends time. Your emphatic 'No' only proves the power of their transgenerational strings that tie your souls together."[6]

Rather than deny the existence of soul wounds, we invite you to go on a journey of soul exploration. The goal here is not to assign blame, but rather to find out the truth about ourselves. The Scripture says, "You will know the truth, and the truth will set you free" (John 8:32 NIV). Finding the truth about our childhood soul wounds allows us to look honestly at our adult relationship patterns and begin to heal them. Healing is our goal, not blame.

Blame Is Not Our Game

One of the biggest hurdles we must jump over as we begin to examine our family of origin is that of accusing or blaming our parents for our current relationship struggles. Many people have trouble looking at their parents with a critical eye. They become protective and do not want to see the negative in their family of origin. The problem with this overly protective stance is that it can cause people not to see the truth about their childhood.

The truth is there is no such thing as a perfect childhood, and there is no such thing as a perfect parent. Romans 3:23 says, "All have sinned and fall short of the glory of God" (NIV). Even the best intended parents have fallen short in some ways. Most families will have lived and behaved in some way (even if it was in accord with the social mores of the time) that impacted their children negatively. Most people will have experienced some kind of pain in childhood. Many will have scars. If this is so, then they must be willing to examine their past, deal with the wounds, and heal that pain so that they can be healthy in their adult relationships.

In understanding and evaluating our family-of-origin issues, our goal is to understand our childhood programming, with mother and father as the primary teachers, who taught us based upon their own possibly faulty learning. We do this without casting any blame or condemnation upon them. They were, after all, only living out their own family-of-origin programming. We, too, are parents, trying to raise our children in the best manner that we know how, and we do not want our children to put us under condemnation, as well.

In looking at the part our family of origin plays in wounding us, we are also not advocating a lack of personal responsibility for our own actions, nor are we saying that our current bad behaviors are our parent's fault. We encourage everyone to take responsibility for their own unhealthy behavior. Understanding where and how we learned to behave in dysfunctional ways is our main goal.

When an individual can trace the inception of certain dysfunctional behaviors, he or she can then take responsibility for accepting and changing his or her actions. We must be willing to examine our behaviors objectively, without denial or blame. Evaluating our childhood and the behavior patterns we learned there with honesty, openness, and forgiveness can, on the other hand, give us a great deal of freedom and spontaneity in our adult relationships. This is exactly what happened with Mike and Carol, the couple you read about earlier in this chapter.

Mike and Carol's Healing

With our help, both Mike and Carol learned a great deal about their unconscious mind and their soul in pain. By revealing and experiencing the effects of their childhood wounds, they gained wisdom and insight that began to free their souls. One day in our office, Mike opened up about his painful past and began to weep for the first time since his grandmother had died so many years before. Carol held him as he recounted forgotten memories of a lost childhood filled with pain. He realized that he had been forever looking for a soft, loving mother figure only to become suspicious, distant, and untrusting once he found her. In this way, he was unconsciously reliving his abandonment wound, and creating an environment that was more familiar to him—unhealthy but familiar nonetheless. These insights gave Mike tremendous awareness about his current behavior patterns with Carol.

They both labored diligently to establish a deep soul healing love they had never before thought possible. They took our advice and decided to face their painful past, so that they could, together, heal their wounds. Their work paid off, enabling them to move from wounding each other to healing each other's souls. It was a love they had always wanted.

As you can probably see, by asking yourself some painfully honest questions about your childhood upbringing, you can begin to gather valuable information about your past and present relationships. Virtually all of the conscious and unconscious information about these patterns is stored in the soul. Accessing the information will greatly aid you in unlearning negative patterns and soul impressions and relearning new and healthy behaviors. The next chapter gives you very easy-to-perform tools to help you retrieve information that may be locked in your unconscious, and thus give you powerful ways to attend to your soul and the soul of your marriage.

CHAPTER 4

ATTENDING THE SOUL

*P*eter came into our counseling center because he was forty-three years old and had been married three times. He was having trouble with his third wife, Emily, and said that they could not see eye to eye on much of anything. He said that Emily would not tolerate his influence and wanted to do everything her way. When I (Tom) questioned him about his previous marriages, he said that he typically picked women who were adversarial and contentious, and Emily was no exception.

"Peter," I asked, "what is your impression or idea of women?"

"What?" he replied, almost offended. "What do you mean, what do I think of women? I love women! I wouldn't have been married three times if that were not true."

I responded by saying that when we see a relationship pattern such as his, there may be deeper issues inside a person that need attending. I suggested that these issues may have to do with Peter's impressions of women locked deep within the soul.

As Peter continued in therapy, he began to look at the guts of his psyche, and he soon discovered that he had an unconscious idea or notion of women that was not so positive. This started with his feelings about his own mother. While he loved his mother very much, and described her as good and loving, he also realized that she was controlling and somewhat suffocating. He was a pleaser and never wanted to disappoint her.

This further aggravated his sense of suffocation, because he felt guilty if he was different, if he did not always succumb to her control. From this realization, Peter determined that he had an unconscious idea that all women would control and oppress him, so he had to constantly maintain power over situations and get his way in order to avoid this. His negative soul impressions were sabotaging his relationships with women and were about to destroy his marriage with Emily.

Soul Impressions

We call Peter's notions and feelings about women *soul impressions*. These are feelings or impressions that exist as a result of the way your family's generational pattern has consciously and unconsciously programmed you. You may have little or no concrete knowledge of this, but your family of origin has affected you nonetheless.

For example, you, like me (Bev), may have an impression within your soul that marriage typically ends in divorce. I got this notion from the programming of all of the divorces in my family that occurred in generations before me. You may have been programmed in much the same way. The problem with soul impressions is that when you least expect it, they may rear their ugly heads and you will find yourself responding to them without even knowing it. Many people enter marriage with negative soul impressions that have left a deep scar on their souls.

In our souls lie the conscious and unconscious information about how we view men, women, religion, life, marriage, God, and countless other issues. It is a database that has been collecting information over a lifetime. Often you are not consciously aware that this information even exists until your views become challenged in some way. This chapter will show you how to access this important information in order to become aware of soul impressions that are buried deep within your soul. This will teach you a great deal about your current belief systems and relationship patterns.

Examining the Soul's Data

In order to better understand how soul impressions impact our love relationships, we must examine more closely the soul's data that has been collected regarding love. Once again let's look at the relationship between Tom and me. I grew up seeing love as difficult, violent, and ending in tragedy. Cognitively, I learned from Scripture and other material that love was good and right and true, but my soul impression was very negative. Because of this, the notion of marriage created a great deal of anxiety for me.

Tom was raised in a Christian home, so he had heard sermons and lectures about the wonders of love between lifetime partners. However, he grew up watching his parents struggle in their marriage and finally divorce, which created a very negative soul impression within him. Now, take these two hopeful romantics, with all of their knowledge, training, and education on healthy relationships, and you would think you could get two successful soul healing lovers. Unfortunately, this was not the case. Our negative soul impressions wreaked havoc on our positive cognitions of love and marriage. Our soul impressions won out over our head knowledge of love, and this left us feeling anxious and fearful in our relationship.

Love Begets Fear and Panic

When an individual is in doubt, panic, or crisis, we believe that soul impressions will win over cognitive knowledge every time. When you are in a state of anxiety, most often your gut will win over your head. Therefore, no matter how many books you read, seminars you attend, or sermons you sit through, you still have to battle your negative soul impressions. They can effectively counteract all of your positive information and training. It is no wonder that adult children of pain and dysfunction have so much trouble with matrimony.

This dilemma has caused us to set out on a journey to relearn or readjust an individual's negative soul impressions toward a much more positive view of love and marriage. To do this, we must examine how the human brain works in collecting soul data.

The Old and New Brain

In Ornstein and Sobel's book *The Healing Brain*, we learn how the brain functions to aid in the compiling of information within our souls. We see that the human brain is divided into two basic parts—the cerebral cortex, which we will call the *new brain*, and the brain stem, which we will refer to as the *old brain*.[1]

Humans are the only mammals that have a new brain. It is the part of the brain that helps us take in information, organize it, and make decisions. It gives us the ability to observe ourselves and evaluate our own behavior. The difference between humans and animals is that we can objectively critique and assess what we do. I can't picture my dog barking frantically at the paper boy and then thinking, "I'll bet I really looked stupid doing that." Sometimes when we do something really embarrassing such as "losing it" in the grocery store because the checker is entirely too slow, the gift of seeing ourselves in our mind's eye may not be so wonderful after all. But we have the ability to do just that.

Beneath the new brain lies the brain stem, or old brain. Cradled at the root of the brain stem is the limbic system, which is our survival mechanism. This primitive old brain is a part of our autonomic nervous system, or our fight-or-flight response. It floods our body with chemicals when it senses real or perceived fear or danger. Painful memories from childhood can trigger the old brain's fight-or-flight response. When our autonomic nervous system kicks in, we have physiological triggers such as sweaty palms, heart palpitations, and perspiration.

Another key aspect about the old brain is that it is atemporal, which means that it has no sense of time. So a trauma that occured at age five can be relived at age twenty-five with the same feeling and emotion that you felt as a child. If you do not believe this, take a minute and think about something you got sick on as a child. Do you eat it today? The answer is typically "NO." Every time we ask this question in Soul Healers Workshops, people give us the names of their food nemeses.

Mine (Bev's) was salmon croquettes. When I was eight years old, I got deathly ill eating them. Until that time I loved them. They were my favorite food. But since I got food poisoning, I still cannot eat them to this day. I try, and just as I get them close to my mouth, I have a severe aversion response and react with a resounding "Yuck!" Now I know in my new brain that salmon croquettes are delicious, but the trauma that is lodged in my old brain keeps me from enjoying my once-favorite delicacy.

I had a client who, as a child, burned her hand on a potbellied stove. This was quite frightening to her because her parents were out drinking, and there was no one there to care for her. To this day she has a serious aversion to these stoves and will not even allow her husband to buy a wood-burning stove for their home. Her irrational, deep-seated feeling about stoves is what we call an "old brainer." It is obvious to most of us in this day and age that wood-burning stoves are not dangerous, but my client is not using her rational thought processes. Her interminable limbic system has been kicked into overdrive. Thus, an "old brainer" has occurred.

The Old Brain and Relationships

As we have seen, many of us can have problems in the present that have their root in past trauma. While "old brainers" may not seem so serious when it comes to potbellied stoves or salmon croquettes, having such negative feelings and sensations about love can be very interpersonally perilous in marriage.

In my own life, love was recorded in my old brain as dangerous and even deadly. To me, love meant pain, abuse, and abandonment. Unfortunately, my old brain fed my very negative soul impression of love. Let me share a personal example with you.

I grew up in the hills of Tennessee, which is a nice way of saying we were "hillbillies," or more commonly known as "rednecks." When I was a young girl, I would listen to my parents fight and become anxious and fearful because the conflicts would often result in violence. I often described my parents' redneck fights as an episode of the television show *Cops*, only without the cops. Typically, the show features redneck parents with flesh grinding and blood spurting and pitiful, traumatized children huddling in the corner frozen in fear. Sadly, this was my childhood.

Often in these redneck fights, my father would threaten to leave. He had done this many times before, but one night when I was five years old, they had a particularly bad redneck fight in which my father said he was going to leave, and I somehow knew he meant it. He told my mother that he could not take her crazy behavior anymore and he was going to leave. All of a sudden, I knew he was serious. All I could think about was that my mother was not normal. She said and did crazy violent things, and I panicked at the thought of being left alone with her and having to take care of my younger siblings. I feared for our safety.

In my panic, I grabbed my father's leg and clung to it for dear life. I begged and pleaded with him to stay. In his angst, he drug me across the wood floor, opened the screen to the porch, and slung me off, saying, "Sorry, kiddo, I'm outta here." I can still feel some of the original old brain trauma of embedding my fingernails in the screen door and begging, through sobs, for my father to come back. He never did, except for limited visits, after that.

I did everything in my power to put this painful memory out of my mind. I was successful for years and thought that I had outrun my negative soul impressions until... I got married.

Years later, as a budding bride of two months, I was so excited as I prepared dinner for my new groom. There is a saying in the deep south, "We are as poor as Job's turkey," which accurately described us as honeymooners. We were both in graduate school and lived from paycheck to paycheck. I was so proud of myself because I had prepared Tom a delicious, nutritious dinner for only $1.88. That economical meal happened to be quiche. Proverbs 31 women had nothing on me as I thought I was truly the ideal bride.

Unfortunately, a book came out in the early 1970s that quickly became a thorn in my side. The name of that book was *Real Men Don't Eat Quiche*. I want to find this clever author someday and tell him just how I feel about his literary contribution and the trouble it caused me in my early marriage.

As I prepared the food, Tom started making faces, curling his lip, and asking what I put in the quiche. He began to tell me about his distaste for mushy egg dishes. Now, as he tells the story in workshops, he says that this had nothing to do with him being a "real man" at all. His honest impression of quiche is that it looks like something that was eaten once and someone brought it back up, baked it, and tried to eat it again. Usually this gets a "yuck" response from the audience, which further proves his point.

As we sat at the kitchen table discussing quiche, our conversation took a bad turn. The conversation turned into an argument, and Tom got heated and said, "I'm leaving. I'm gonna go out on the porch and cool off."

When he was young, his mother told him that all good, hot-blooded Portuguese boys should cool off when they get mad. His mother taught him, in lieu of losing his temper and hurting someone's feelings, to go outside and calm down. One would think that I, his bride, would see the healthy rationale in this—but no! I had a major "old brainer."

"Leave! ... Did I hear you say *leave*?" The danger bell rang in the limbic factory of my old brain, and there I was, anxious, panicked, full of the fear of death. I clung. I cried. I grabbed his leg. "Please don't leave. How could you be so mean as to leave me at a time like this?!"

"Huh?" he sighed incredulously. "What are you so upset about? I'm just cooling off like my mom taught me years ago! Can't a guy get a break around here?"

My old brain did not want to give Tom a break, and my negative soul impressions told me that when a man leaves, he may not come back. At that point, I was not thinking like a young, sensible bride. I was thinking like an abandoned little girl. It was very difficult for Tom and me that night. Needless to say, our honeymoon haven had been disrupted by a terrible old brainer. I learned later that there was name for my overreaction. It is called *reactivity*.

Reactivity

The definition of *reactivity* is to use more emotion in a current situation than it deserves because a soul wound is being triggered. As we stated earlier, many painful memories of our past are stored in the old brain. These memories can be triggered and activated by stimuli in our present relationships. Let's say that your mother was very lax in preparing food for you as a child. Let's also assume that your wife forgot to pack your lunch as you were leaving for work. You may have one of many responses. You may tell her that you are disappointed, and you request that she do better in the future. You may also just overlook it and decide to eat out with your associates. But if you overreact, get enraged, yell, threaten, accuse, or pout, then you are experiencing reactivity.

Old Brainers and Marital Strife

One of the things we learned the hard way as we dealt with reactivity in our early marriage is that if one mate becomes reactive, then there is a greater likelihood that he or she will trigger reactivity in their partner. This is what happened with us when we dealt with what we now call the "quiche affair."

When I overreacted to Tom's leaving that night as we argued over quiche, I triggered reactivity in him. He will tell you his story. I (Tom) grew up in a Christian home and had a pretty good childhood until I was thirteen years old and I discovered that my father was having an affair with a nurse at our family doctor's office. I told my mom, and my dad was furious with me and blamed me for the conflict that ensued. We called the pastor, our youth leader, and a couple of elders in our church to come over and try to help my parents patch things up. They managed to stick together just barely, but my dad never got over his anger at me, and my mom never trusted my dad again.

They stayed together for the next eleven years, but they were never close again. My mom began to confide in me and tell me what a poor Christian and bad husband my father was. I wanted to be there for her, but her constant clinging and neediness was suffocating to me. I could not wait to graduate and go to college just to get away from her constant smothering. I, like Bev, thought that I could outrun those painful feelings of being clung to... until the fateful night of the "quiche affair."

When I left the room to cool off, Bev reacted to her childhood soul wound of abandonment by begging, pleading, and clinging for me to return. Unfortunately, this triggered my soul wound of being suffocated and clung to by my mom. I overreacted and felt the overwhelming urge to escape. Bev's reactivity triggered my reactivity and both of us were severely overreacting. We call this phenomenon *interactivity*.

Interactivity

Knowing what we know about the power of "old brainers" to bring destruction to couples, it is easy to see how these experiences can become volatile. We often see that one partner, for example, the wife, becomes fearful, angry, and overly emotional, which causes her to draw false conclusions about her husband. Her husband will then become angry and fearful and hurl a few false accusations of his own.

Dr. Patricia Love calls this, "Making up your own reality about your partner."[3] As you can see, I had made up my own reality that Tom would leave me. I drew a false conclusion that he would do as other men had done in my past. Tom assumed that I wanted to suffocate him and cling to him, and so he wanted to distance himself from me.

Our wounds were indeed interactive, and both of our responses to our own woundedness served to further hurt each other. We were wounding each other in much the same way as our parents had wounded us, and we could not seem to help ourselves. We felt like the apostle Paul in Romans 7:15 when he said, "I do not understand what I do. For what I want to do, I do not do, but what I hate I do" (NIV).

One of my greatest fears was that Tom would leave me, yet my hysterics could actually facilitate this reality. My reactivity could have actually made it hard for him to stay. I was doing that which I hated, because I was responding out of my fear and creating a struggle for my husband, and he in turn did the same.

Family Ghosts and Negative Soul Impressions

Making up our own reality about our partner is similar to what Transgenerational Therapists call the phenomenon of *family ghosts*. The theory is that the "ghosts" of our parents, siblings, and ex-partners show up in current relationships. Transgenerational therapists use the term "putting someone else's face on your spouse." When I was fearful of Tom leaving me, I was "putting my father's abandoning face on him." Putting the faces of past "ghosts" on current relationships can lead to trouble. Take Ann Marie for example.

Ann Marie's Family Ghosts

Ann Marie came to the counseling center because she was struggling in her two-year relationship with Donald. There were times when she felt a great deal of love for Donald, but at other times, her feelings would shift so quickly that she would break the relationship off in a panic. Later, she would come to her senses and reunite with him. She came to counseling to determine, once and for all, if Don was the one for her, and to see if they could make it as a successful married couple.

When I questioned her about her childhood, I found that she was the oldest child of three girls. Her father, a local orthodontist, was a very critical man, and seemed to feel responsible to straighten out all his daughters' lives, as well as their teeth. Dad constantly criticized Ann Marie and her sisters, and belittled them in public. Whenever she would bring home her report card, Dad would first notice what was lacking: "Ann Marie, what is this A- in Latin? You should be able to make an A+." Because of this, Ann Marie never felt that she measured up to her dad, or in any of her relationships for that matter.

Upon further questioning about her relationship with Donald, Ann Marie told me that he was also very critical. She shared with me several instances in which he told her what spice to use in the chili, or that she had a dry spot on her nose so perhaps she should put some lotion on it. I could not say with absolute certainty that Don was well-meaning in his motives, but to me these statements did not appear to be criticism, as much as merely helpful comments. It seems that Ann Marie was so sensitive to measuring up that she was putting her father's face on Donald when he would give her simple, helpful advice.

This caused her to become reactive to Donald's perceived criticism. Her reactivity caused him to react, and interactivity was fully operational in their relationship. They both needed to take a deeper look at themselves.

Accessing Information in the Soul

From Ann Marie's example, we learned that people can have very well-honed defense mechanisms to prevent them from feeling their pain. Many times we, as counselors, must help people override those defenses by other means. We have developed a tool that is designed to override your defense mechanisms and allow the Holy Spirit to show you information and patterns that occur within your soul. This tool uses your cognitive as well as subliminal resources to aid in soul reflection. The tool is called the *Soul Healogram*. Here is how it works.

The Soul Healogram

Get in a quiet place. Give yourself forty-five minutes to complete this exercise. Pray and ask the Lord to guide you in accessing your conscious and unconscious memories of your parents, extended family, and ancestors. Tom and I have found Him to be a great soul tour guide as we completed this exercise. Because the space in the book is limited, you may wish to get a much larger piece of paper to do this exercise, and use the outline in the book as a guideline.

On your paper, you will see a large box that represents you; beside it is a box that represents your spouse, if you are married. The boxes just above your box represent your parents. Above them are boxes representing your grandparents on both your mother's and father's side. The small boxes beside your own represent your siblings. The boxes beside your parents represent your paternal and maternal aunts and uncles. If any cousins played a significant role in your life, draw a small box for them, as well.

From this diagram, you will see a transgenerational panorama of your family of origin and descendants. To many of you, the drawing may look some what like a genogram, which is a tool used in social work and family therapy. Write the names of each person above each box. You will see a line in the center of every box. On the top half of the box, write the *negative* characteristics of these family members. On the bottom, write the *positive* characteristics.

You may label and fill in boxes for as many generations as you have information. It is best if you can fill in at least three generations because you will be able to see some patterns repeating themselves in your family. If you do not consciously remember a family member, you may write down what you heard about them from family folklore.

For example, I never knew my maternal grandmother. I heard from various family members that she was worrisome and very passive. She was married to my grandfather, a very violent, cruel alcoholic, who abused her and her children regularly. I frequently heard this particularly sad story about my maternal grandmother.

When she was pregnant with my mother, my grandfather went on a drinking binge and did not come home for weeks. My grandmother had no income, so she began to panhandle and beg for food for herself and her children. The local townspeople took pity on her and would put their leftover cornbread, beans, and fat back out on the lids of their garbage pails so that when she would come by she could have food to eat.

My grandmother constantly worried about money and was always concerned about where her next meal would come from. Learning this information from family folklore gave me tremendous insight into my family and myself, because as long as I could remember, my mother had an inordinate fear of poverty. She constantly feared that she was going to be penniless. What amazed me was that as far back as I could trace, I also had a deep-seated fear that I was not going to have enough money to make ends meet. Many times there was no logical rationale for this fear. In learning about my grandmother, I realized that many of her fears were passed down to my mother and eventually to me, yet there was no reasonable explanation for us to entertain them. I now know that I had a very negative soul impression about money that was passed down to me through my family, and I was not consciously aware that this had happened.

These soul impressions can be the result of "curses" that are passed down generationally, much like diseases and other hereditary conditions. Exodus 20:5–6 says, "I, the Lord your God, am a jealous God, visiting the iniquity of the fathers upon the children to the third and fourth generations of those who hate Me, but showing mercy to thousands, to those who love Me and keep My commandments" (NKJV). Apparently, these "curses" or patterns had been visited upon my family for three generations.

As you complete the following exercise, you may see these unexplainable patterns or "curses" within your own family. This insight can be very beneficial for the healing of your soul.

Take some time now and complete the **Soul Healogram** on the following pages.

The Soul Healogram

Draw your family tree as far back as you can remember. Write the names of each person at the top of each box. List the negative characteristics at the top of the boxes, and the positive characteristics at the bottom. List all soul impressions beside each box.

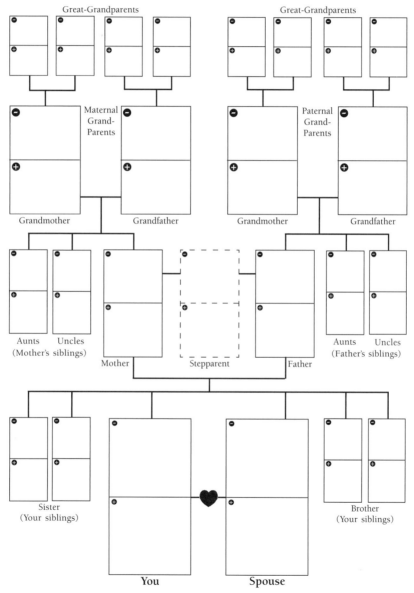

From Soul-Healing Love by Drs. Beverly and Tom Rodgers ©2006 Drs. Beverly and Tom Rodgers

The Soul Healogram Part Two Instructions

When you have completed all the boxes in Part One, you are ready to move on to Part Two of this exercise. Look at the boxes for patterns of behavior, repetitive characteristics, or occurrences that you might notice. As I (Bev) share my insights about my Soul Healogram with you, it may help you see some patterns of your own.

As I completed the Soul Healogram, I saw that all of the men on my mother's side were addicted to alcohol, drugs, or gambling (many to all three). There was a great deal of mental illness, and everyone (I mean *everyone*) was divorced. I also saw that the men on both sides were weak and did not take the leadership role in their marriages. In contrast, the women were very strong and, by default, had to lead their families. Most of these women were codependent and miserable, which is why I am sure their marriages ended in divorce. These patterns programmed my psyche as I grew up. They left soul impressions that affected me as an adult.

Is it any wonder that as a wife, I could not trust my husband's leadership? I constantly felt like I had to be the strong one and do everything on my own. In my new brain, I knew that my husband was a strong, capable leader, but my old brain kept me from believing this and living it out. This story illustrates how this affected the Rodgers' honeymoon haven.

We had been married for about three months, and I asked Tom to take the bills to the post office and mail them. Now growing up, there were several times when my family did not pay the gas bill or the water bill. I would come home from school and dread seeing the notes on our front door because I just knew that we would be without power or water. Once again, I repressed these memories and thought that all of this was in the past.

As a dutiful husband, Tom agreed to take the bills to the post office. But when I came home early from work that day, I saw that they were still there. In my new brain, I knew that there was a reasonable explanation for his behavior. Perhaps he had planned to come by in the afternoon and pick them up for the later mail drop. Maybe he knew of a mailbox that was closer and would drop them there after work. But my old brain began to work on me. Tom came home about ten minutes later, and I lit into him, saying things like, "Why can't I trust you? Why do I feel like I have to do everything around here? My mother was right. Men are undependable. I should never have married you. Maybe I'd have been better off not trusting anyone!"

I remember the feeling of actually engaging my new brain and thinking—you are overreacting. But I could not help myself. I continued to rail at Tom for what I perceived as his extreme untrustworthiness. (Hmm… I wonder where this came from? The answer can be found in my Soul Healogram.)

Sadly, my old brain kicked in, and my soul wounds were triggered as I thought that Tom was like most of the men in my family of origin who could not be counted on to be responsible leaders. Because of this feeling, I became very reactive. This reactivity and criticism caused Tom to react, and there we were, embroiled in interactivity… again.

In designing the Soul Healogram, I could clearly see how my family of origin programmed me to think and react the way I did in my marriage. I cannot tell you how helpful it was for me to see that I was not hysterical, mean, or just plain nuts. I was simply programmed for generations to react this way, and now that I knew the problem, I could allow the Lord to solve it.

The wonderful thing about the Soul Healogram is that it can point out information about repetitive family patterns that can be very insightful. This tool can also show you reasons for certain behaviors that you indulge in that previously you could not logically explain.

As you complete the Soul Healogram, take a yellow highlighter and find all the similarities you can see in the positive and negative characteristics of your family members. List these at the bottom of the page. As you do this, you will likely see common characteristics or themes develop. When you have finished, complete the outline on the following pages.

As you complete the sentences in Part Two of this exercise, it is important that you answer these questions from your old brain and not your new brain. In other words, do not answer with your head, but answer from your gut.

When we do our Soul Healers Weekends, we tell couples that if they take more than three seconds to answer each question, then they are doing it wrong. The answers to the questions in Part Two of the Soul Healogram should only take a few seconds. This way you can be sure that you are answering from your "bowels" and expressing the depth of your soul. Take a few minutes and answer the following questions.

THE SOUL HEALOGRAM Part Two
From my Soul Healogram, I learned that ...

Men in my family are_____

_____

Women in my family are_____

_____

Marriage in my family is _____

_____

Conflict in my family is_____

_____

Communication in my family is_____

_____

Coping in my family is_____

_____

Feelings in my family are_____

_____

The addictive patterns in my family are_____

_____

In my family, divorce is_____

_____

In my family, abuse is _____

_____

In my family, religion is_____

_____

In my family, God is_____

_____

Based on the data that I have collected, I have an inner belief

that marriage is_____

_____

_____

and that my mate is _____

_____

_____

As I learn to heal the wounds of my family and society, I would

like my idea of marriage to be:_____

_____

_____

I am reactive to the following issues:_____

_____

_____

The soul wounds that I would like to heal are_____

_____

_____

The following are my Soul Healing goals:_____

_____

_____

_____

_____

_____

_____

Now that you have accessed some very important data from your unconscious, you are ready to begin the soul healing process. The next chapter is dedicated to how this process can take place.

CHAPTER 5

THE SOUL IN HEALING

*N*ow that you have completed the Soul Healogram in the previous chapter, you may be surprised at what is buried deep within your unconscious mind. You will be able to see a cross section of your unconscious, so that you can bring these insights to the forefront of your conscious mind. There are many realizations that you will make after reviewing the data on your Soul Healogram. You may, for example, see that many of the men in your family were critical and controlling. As a result, you have a tendency to over-interpret your spouse's behavior as critical or controlling, when this may only be partially true. It may be apparent to you that most of the women in your family were passive enablers. Because of this, you may either become too passive in your marriage, or compensate by being too controlling.

As you gain these types of insights about your soul, it is important to set goals that move you and your mate toward healing. The best way to do this is to write these goals down. We encourage couples to sit down together and write what we call a Soul Healing Plan, which is the last part of the Soul Healogram. This plan will include individual goals, as well as couple goals for your relationship. Each goal should be doable, in that they are realistic, and they should be quantifiable, or able to tabulate or record.

This is important because many people come into counseling thinking that they know what they want but are unable to determine exactly what that is or how to measure it. We often ask couples to also write down what achieving their goals might look like so that they can get a clearer picture of what they want.

Dual Tracks of Soul Healing

The Soul Healing Plan should have your personal goals, or the things that you would like to work on within yourself, as well as goals for your marriage. We have noticed that people often want to set marital goals and list all the things that they want their mate to change. Yet they do not want to look at what they can do to heal their own soul wounds.

These people have no idea about how to nurture their own soul. They in turn project their lack of happiness onto their spouses. They blame their partners for the emptiness within their souls. This can be very deadly for a marriage because people think that all of their personal problems or soul problems are marital problems. In other words, they blame much of their unhappiness on their marriage relationship and do not consider that they could be unhappy inside. This is why there are two tracks to soul healing. The first is to look at your own soul wounds, old brainers, and reactivity and write goals for you to deal with them and allow the Lord to heal them in your own life. The second is to use the tools and techniques in the Model to heal your marriage. In order to help people move toward individual soul healing, we have put together some ideas that can be helpful. Many of these can be included in one's Soul Healing Plan.

Individual Soul Healing Goals

Over the years, we have put together a list of some ways that not only have brought about soul healing for Tom and I, but have also been helpful for many people we have treated in counseling. We thought it would be helpful for us to share some of these soul healing experiences with you.

One of the ways to heal one's soul is to begin to listen to the soul and pay attention to what it is trying to tell you. The concept of listening to the soul is discussed in great detail in Thomas Moore's *The Care of the Soul*. Moore makes a wonderfully strong case for slowing down and attending to the soul. The following are a sampling of suggestions of soul healing activities that are designed to attend to the soul.

Soul Healing through Meditation and Prayer

There are many pathways to listening to the soul. Prayer and meditation are two significant ways. Through them we can not only listen to ourselves, but we can also hear from God. There are times when I (Bev) have been silent before God and He began to tell me what my soul needs were before I even realized it. Silence can be a very good way to attend to the soul. I have a friend who facilitates silent retreats in which no one speaks for the entire weekend. Many participants report astounding spiritual renewal. Some even say they hear the voice of God for the very first time.

Soul Healing through Therapy

Therapy can be a wonderful way to care for the soul. Tom and I haven't always been people helpers. Once we sat at the feet of great soul healers. We, too, were clients of therapy. I am grateful for the many hours that I have spent with healers, as I poured out stories of painful scenes from my childhood. Their merciful Christlike guidance showed me the way to heal my soul. It was the love of spiritual leaders and mentors, as well as the mercy and insight of unconditionally loving therapists, that began to transform my soul and create a positive vision of love in my life.

Soul Healing through Self-Parenting

For people who grew up with alcoholic, abusive, or mentally ill parents, completing the Soul Healogram can be very eye-opening, but also painful. They see clearly that they were not supported, nurtured, or cared for in many areas as a child. These people can be greatly healed by practicing self-parenting. Basically, this is developing a relationship with yourself that is positive and supportive rather than judging yourself harshly and putting yourself down. Learning to do the things for your soul that a mother or father would do can be very soul healing.

Soul Healing through Nature

I have always been a busy person. In graduate school, I would run from place to place in a busy flurry, often not noticing whether it was a sunny or rainy day. Certainly, I never noticed the flowers or the trees. I thought I did not have time for nature or God's creation. I had places to go, papers to write, and people to help. As I have grown older and become more aware of my soul needs, I have found a very special place in my life for nature. I have even taken up gardening. Never would I have thought that I would like to dig in the dirt like a happy, carefree child, but it is one of the most fulfilling, soul-nurturing activities in my day. Sometimes I get so absorbed in my garden that I completely lose track of time. Often I come inside from a long day in the garden, covered with dirt. I am filthy and completely content. My soul feels happy and fed. Thomas Moore calls this feeling *soulfulness*.[1] I have a sign in my garden that says, "He who plants a garden works hand in hand with God." It is indeed true that the soul can be nourished as the soil is nourished.

Soul Healing through Worship

Worshiping God can be a wonderful experience in soul healing. Praise music offers a soul-connecting experience with our Creator. Worship reminds us that God is constantly in and through all of creation. It is our human response to God's ever-present love. Through praise and worship, there can be a rapturous feeling of oneness between God and humankind, but worship can be difficult for some people.

As marital and family therapists, we have days when we hear the problems of today's families, and our compassion for their pain often causes us to feel a deep burden. We call this a "soul weight." We have a saying on these days that "we have heard too much." You may have had these kinds of days, too. Your neighbor confides in you that she wants to leave her husband. You hear from the prayer chain that an infant has cancer. Your child comes home with a story of betrayal from a trusted friend. These are the days when our souls need uplifting. In our home we put on praise music and allow it to minister to us and soothe our souls with God's love and presence.

Soul Healing through Healing Your Inner Child

There is a way to nurture the soul that many people have not thought about in years. This is to remember those things you did as a child that gave your soul wings. Thomas Moore says that a child is the face of soul, and to move against that would cause the soul to suffer.[2] Just take a look at the ways you ignore and even shame your own childlikeness.

Our society believes that people should be mature, strong, and grown up. Any regression to childhood is strongly discouraged. Nevertheless, moving back to the ways of childhood can bring back the lighthearted spirit in many people. Go ahead, find the lost passions of your youth and try them again. Ride a bike. Go on a hike. Play touch football with the whole family. Fly a kite. Build a model plane. Make a mess. It will feel good once you get used to it.

Soul Healing through Laughter and Play

Laughter is a great medicine for the soul. In fact, it is innate in children to laugh and play. For them not to play would mean that they were not normal. But in many dysfunctional families, children are wounded in this area. In these homes, laughter and play are discouraged, and seriousness is actively or passively rewarded. The natural playful instinct of children who grew up in these homes was robbed from them.

These wounded adults heard things like: "Don't act silly" and "Don't make noise." Laughter and play were seen as boisterous and disruptive and, therefore, to be discouraged. These parents would strongly shame their children for this behavior. Some would even punish them for it. This caused these children to split off from their natural state of playfulness. As adults, they became serious and stoic.

This was the case in my (Bev's) home. Consequently, I had to give myself permission to laugh and play. It took a while for me to feel comfortable doing this. But as I learned how to loosen up, laugh, and play, my soul was nurtured and my marriage improved, as well.

Soul Healing through Couple's Play

Laughter and high-energy play (play that gets your heart rate up and allows you to have fun at the same time) can be very good for your soul. Studies show that they can be very bonding for people, as well. Just think about the people you played with on team sports when you grew up. Don't you still feel a sense of connection with them even today?

High-energy play can also be a good bonding experience for couples. It creates a synergy between people that can be very fulfilling. Often we see couples who are in trouble, and they cannot remember the last time they played together. Some say they have even forgotten how to play with their partner.

It has been said that couples who pray together, stay together. Now we add to this that couples who play together, also stay together. Because we think play is so important, we have an entire evening in our fifteen-hour Intensive Soul Healers Weekends dedicated to couple's play. We play games like passing a lifesaver from mouth to mouth with a toothpick, or moving a credit card between your lips by only using puffs of air. Our favorite is what we call the *Orange Game* where you have to pass an orange from one mate's neck to the other without using your hands! These games get people moving, touching, laughing, and having fun. Many of them say that this is the first time they have laughed and played in a long while.

This is particularly sad because research shows that having fun is listed in the top five reasons why people pick their mate. "He or she makes me laugh" is listed in the top ten. This means that couples who have stopped laughing and having fun are moving far away from the positive relationship they once had. This is what happened to Ashley and Brett.

Ashley and Brett's Story of Play

Over twenty years ago, Ashley and Brett came to see me (Bev) to get some help dealing with their teenage sons. Both boys were struggling with drugs and alcohol, and they needed individual and family therapy. Tom was a youth pastor at that time, so I typically asked all of the teens that I worked with if they wanted to be a part of his large, thriving youth group. I know that dual relationships are not encouraged with therapists, but I was much more concerned with getting these boys into a healthy peer group than "covering my ethical behind."

My philosophy paid off because the boys loved to have a group of friends who could have fun without drugs and alcohol. They also learned about God's unconditional love and accepted Christ, which was the main reason they stopped using drugs and alcohol.

The family did great in therapy, and Ashley and Brett even joined the youth staff as parent sponsors. They accompanied us on many trips we took with the youth. This was great for their family and good for our youth group, as well. Ashley was a pure delight and was great at playing with the youth and having fun. She was always organizing games and getting everyone involved. What I remember about her most was that she had this distinctive laugh. Brett would get her tickled, and her laugh was so contagious that the whole group would laugh with them, including me.

The boys grew up, got clean and sober, and the last I heard, they were both doing well in college. About five years ago, I received a call from Brett. He said they he and Ashley were in deep trouble. It seems that after the boys straightened out, he was laid off from his high-paying job. He then started a business that went under, and they moved his alcoholic father in, whom they cared for until he died. They then moved in Ashley's alcoholic mother and cared for her for almost a decade until she died.

Brett said that they survived all of this, but that last year he was laid off *again* from another job. Ashley was still teaching school and wanted to retire but couldn't because of Brett's job loss. It was the last straw for Ashley, and she said that she had had enough; she was tired of striving, and she wanted a divorce. They had been separated for the last year (in our state, you have to have a year of separation before you can file for divorce) but still living in the same house. He lived upstairs, and she lived downstairs. The tension in the house was thick, and the divorce was just about to be finalized.

Fortunately, we shared the same attorney, and he happened to be the boys' godfather. He said that he would only draw up the divorce papers if Brett and Ashley would agree to go to a Soul Healers Couple's Weekend. Up to that point, we had lost touch with Brett and Ashley, and they did not know that we were doing couple's retreats. He called me and said that he would try to get Ashley to come to our next workshop, but he was not sure she was interested in reconciling their marriage. It just so happened that the next workshop was scheduled for the next day. How's that for God's timing?

Brett did convince Ashley to come, mostly to see me again, but she was closed off and miserable. I will never forget how sad she was the first evening of the retreat. All she did was cry. At one point I asked if I could help her in any way, and she said, "I just wish that Brett could treat me as nice as he does our neighbors."

Brett said that the atmosphere in their home was so strained that they were no longer friends and he had a hard time even speaking to her. Yet he did want their marriage to work, so he continually tried to engage Ashley in doing the exercises and talking to him at the workshop. Still she resisted, telling us that she had been through too much for too long and she was simply "out of gas."

Finally, Saturday night came. This is the night in the Soul Healers Workshop when we play. Game night is our favorite time of the workshop because couples snicker, touch, and laugh. We were all playing the Orange Game, when one of the couples squashed their orange. I bent down to get them a new one, and at that moment, I heard it… Ashley's distinctive, contagious laugh.

I looked up to spot her. Just then our eyes met, and we both were thinking the same thing at the same time. We were thinking about how much fun they used to have as a couple in our youth group. Instantly, we read each other's minds like women can do, and we both started to cry. Brett caught on quickly and teared up, as well. I walked toward them, and Brett began hugging her and kissing her on the top of her head. (Brett was six-feet four-inches tall and Ashley was only five-foot-one.) When I approached them, she was whispering through sobs, "I have forgotten how good this was, and I miss it so badly. I miss being 'us.'"

The three of us had a tearful group hug right in the middle of the retreat. From that point on, things began to turn around for Brett and Ashley. They remembered who they were, who their "us" was, and who they could be again, all because they relearned how to play. They left the retreat saying that they were not going to get a divorce and they had renewed hope in their marriage. I gave them the lifetime homework assignment of always laughing and playing, no matter how bad it got, to never forget how good it felt to play.

About a year later, a young couple pushing a stroller approached me at the mall. "Do you remember me?" he asked. It was Brett and Ashley's oldest son, with his wife and small son. They told me about their jobs and children, and filled me in on their life. They also were going to church with Brett and Ashley, who had actually become their young couples' Sunday school class teachers.

Finally the young man's pretty wife said, "Can I ask you a strange question? Were you the one that taught my in-laws that crazy Orange Game?"

"Why?" I asked.

"Because every time we have a Sunday school party, they will not let us do anything else until we play that silly game. They tell us that some wise mentor told them that couples who forget to play will pay. Are you that wise mentor?" she asked.

"I guess I am," was all I could say.

On occasion we still see Brett and Ashley riding their twin Harleys down the streets of our town, enjoying each other and having fun. Obviously, they took what they learned to heart and were putting it to good use.

If your life has gotten so stressful that you, too, have forgotten to play, you might want to follow Brett and Ashley's lead and regularly schedule time to play in your life. If you are like Tom and me, you might have to "work" at play. The important thing is to be intentional and conscious about play. So go ahead, schedule tickle fights, wrestling matches, water gun contests, go-cart races, biking, volleyball, or soccer. Get your heart rate and your connectedness rate higher.

The Soul Healing Plan

When you have assessed the needs of your soul, and written some individual goals down on your Soul Healing Plan, it is then time to start looking at setting goals for your marriage. Let's say that you learned from your Soul Healogram that there were more divorces in your family than stable long-term marriages. You may have an internal belief, or soul impression, that marriages do not last. Possible goals for your Soul Healing Plan may read as follows:

Soul Healing Plan

1-20-2006 Find several couples who have healthy relationships and spend time with them, allowing them to mentor us. This will be done within the next six months.

1-20-2006 Attend a Soul Healers Workshop or marriage enrichment weekend within the next year.

1-22-2006 Read one book on couple's communication together within the next six months.

As you can see, the goals are dated and given a completion time. This helps you and your spouse to assess your progress, as well as stay motivated to accomplish your tasks. When you have completed your goals, plan a surprise or celebration for yourself and your mate to mark out your accomplishment. This will add to your sense of achievement, and encourage you to move even further ahead as a soul healing couple. In order to help you to better understand how to develop your own Soul Healing Plan, we will walk you through how one particular couple developed goals from the information they collected from their Soul Healograms.

Donna and Alex's Soul Healogram

Donna, a tall, thin, frenzied young woman came into our office with Alex, her chubby, laid-back husband. After the birth of their third child, Donna noticed that their marriage had started suffering. Alex seemed to stay longer each day at his job as an insurance underwriter. Donna would complain and nag him to pay more attention to her and the children. He, in turn, would say he was working so much to make things better for their growing family.

Donna felt abandoned and alone, and Alex felt pressured and unappreciated. This is a very common marital struggle we see regularly in counseling: one mate wants closeness, and the other wants distance. Of course, they are attracted to each other. Remember, couples with similar wounds and opposite adaptations to those wounds find each other, and it is typical for individuals caught in such struggles to think that they have picked the wrong mate.

"I should just find a man who wants to spend time with his family," Donna said.

"I should have picked a career woman, who would understand my vocational drive and get off my back," Alex groaned.

We encouraged them to set some soul healing goals and be patient and allow the Lord to bring healing through this process. We also said that there was indeed hope for Alex, and that we had treated many couples in their situation, with very favorable outcomes.

One of the things we know from our research is that many people who divorce pick similar mates the second (or third) time around. This is because there are certain unconscious factors related to whom we select for a mate. We told Donna that if she left Alex, there was a great possibility that she would not be attracted to a clinging male who wanted to spend all of his time with her. Opposites attract. There is a huge likelihood that she would be in the same boat with yet another partner, who had the same basic wounds and issues as Alex. We encouraged her to "dance with the one what brung ya," as my southern grandmother used to say. She would tell me stories about the barn dances in the hills of Tennessee. She said that you could get in a lot of trouble if you did not dance with the boy you came with. In other words, before you get off the dance floor or find another dance partner, stay with your original one and give the dance a chance. Donna and Alex started their dance by completing the Soul Healogram and developing a Soul Healing Plan.

In her Soul Healogram, Donna saw that the women in her family, especially on her mom's side, were caretakers who appeared to be the glue that kept the families together. She noticed a pattern of aloof, distant men on her father's side, starting with her paternal grandfather and moving down the genetic line to her father, her uncle, and her own brother. Almost all of the couples on both sides of her family appeared to have marriages she would describe as functional, but remote and detached. For this reason, Donna never enjoyed family reunions because all of the married couples seemed so miserable. Early in life she started desiring to have a happy marriage and be very different from the rest of her family.

Donna had an interesting insight about her parents' marriage. Although nothing was ever said, she had a soul impression that her father was unfaithful to her mother. She concluded that the guilt of this undiscovered affair was one of the reasons her father stayed so distant from her mother. She had a fear that her own marriage would be like theirs. Because of these insights, she realized that she had placed very high expectations on her husband regarding how much time he spent with her and the children. She realized that she would become reactive if he became distant in any way. She shared this insight with Alex. Her brave and honest confession of this insight made Alex soften at her candor and lack of defensiveness.

Alex made some realizations of his own while completing his Soul Healogram. It was not surprising to us that he found the women in his family to be clingy, whiny, and very dependent. The men, on the other hand, were dominant, controlling, and distant. He saw that his own parent's marriage was a replica of his maternal grandparents, who were unhappily married for fifty-two years. The main thing he remembered about his grandparents' relationship was that they criticized each other constantly. He could see that his own parents were heading down that path.

In his Soul Healogram, Alex saw women, especially his mother, as suffocating and needy. He admitted that he had a tendency to become reactive to this and see Donna in this same light. We pointed out that he would be inclined to "make up" that his wife was clingy, even when her request for closeness was legitimate. He could also put his mother's suffocating face on Donna and see her as another version of his mother. We tell couples that they will see their partner as they saw their care-takers because their unconscious eye is "trained" to do so.

Both Donna and Alex began to see the "catch-me-if-you-can" game they had been playing during their marriage. With Alex not wanting to be engulfed, and Donna not wanting to be abandoned, they both played a part in keeping intimacy just out of reach. Both were dealing with reactivity and negative soul impressions that they projected onto each other. As Alex and Donna saw their patterns more clearly, they were able to set goals to improve their marriage. Here is an example of how they did this.

Alex and Donna's Soul Healing Plan

Donna and Alex started by setting a goal to begin individual therapy to help deal with their family-of-origin patterns. Alex started counseling with Tom, and Donna came to see me. They did this right away. Another goal they set was to attend a Soul Healers Workshop within the next three months. With a little help from us, they set up date nights every other week that focused on having fun, talking, playing, and connecting. Alex agreed to give Donna the present of taking fifteen minutes at the end of every other day and allowing her to share about her day, as he maintained eye contact and focused attention solely on her. This did wonders for her need for closeness. Donna agreed to give Alex a present of lecture-free, nag-free evenings.

When they did get their alone time, it was no longer going to be a time to complain, whine, beg, or lecture Alex on what he did not do or needs he did not meet.Donna was to commit to be positive and grateful.

The game of marital "catch me if you can" began to cease as they started this process. Donna learned to make clear requests and share her feelings and needs in a non-suffocating fashion. By learning to openly ask for what she wanted without feeling guilty, Donna stopped whining and clinging to justify her needs to Alex. This made life for Alex more pleasant, and thus he wanted to meet her needs more often. The tension in their relationship began to subside, and things became more livable for both of them.

So that you can get a better idea of how to set your own soul healing goals, we will show you a sampling of Alex and Donna's Soul Healing Plan.

Alex will start bi-monthly individual therapy with Dr. Tom 1-25-2006.

Donna will start bi-monthly individual therapy with Dr. Bev 1-25-2006.

We both will attend a Soul Healers Workshop within the next three months.

We will focus on learning communication techniques and use them at least twice a week, starting now.

Alex will work on not withdrawing or shutting down while Donna is talking, starting now.

Donna will work on not lecturing, criticizing, or whining when discussing something with Alex, starting now.

We will have date nights every other week, preferably on Saturday. During the dates we will take turns picking fun things to do that will create bonding between us. Alex will start first on 2-14-2006.

We will share with each other any significant insights we gain from our individual therapy, as well as continue in marital therapy for six months until we feel like we have a handle on the issues that need healing within our marriage.

As you can see, Alex and Donna's counseling has gone beyond the typical deal-making, tit-for-tat, quid-pro-quo type of counseling that many receive. So often couples come to counseling with the goal of getting even or rebalancing the power in the relationship. Many times we, as counselors, feel like grade-school teachers with tattling children trying to get us to take sides, scold their partner, or make trades, rather than marriage counselors trying to heal the souls of couples.

Donna and Alex moved beyond this "if-she-does-this-then-he'll-do-that" type of relationship. Their goal became to understand each other, minister to each other, give each other presents, and *agape* each other with God's help. Their aim was to move from soul wounders to soul healers.

One of the changes that Donna noticed first was that her tendency to judge Alex's motives harshly began to subside. After seeing him struggle and work through his Soul Healogram, she started to envision Alex as wounded, and thus developed empathy for him where there once was criticism and control. This helped her to stop clinging, controlling, and nagging, and to start calmly asking for what she needed. She began to get a clearer picture of who Alex was without all of her added projections and reactivity. The insight and help Donna received from her Soul Healogram was very profitable, but she needed additional help to heal her previous image of Alex.

Donna still had trouble believing that Alex really wanted to be close to her. She was haunted by the feeling that he was only doing the exercises because a counselor told him to. She feared that the "old Alex" would eventually appear again and ruin all of the progress they had made. To heal these haunting feelings that couples have as they are trying to heal, we developed an exercise that specifically deals with this stubborn type of fear. This exercise is called the *True Vision Exercise*.

This exercise is designed to help individuals who have a particularly bad or negative image of their partner begin to see him or her through God's eyes. This technique helps couples get a vision of who their partner can be in the Lord, and it also helps neutralize the reactivity that comes from the soul wounds of the past. The tendency for a person to put the unhealthy faces of their caretakers on their spouse can be alleviated by using this tool. Donna and Alex learned to get a true, clear vision of each other after completing this exercise. Here is how they did this.

True Vision Exercise

Donna and Alex examined the list of all the commonalities they saw on their Soul Healogram. These included patterns, characteristics, and soul impressions. They determined what conclusions they had drawn or beliefs they had formulated as a result of living in their families. Both of them wrote all of these beliefs in a column on the left-hand side of their page, which they entitled "BELIEFS." They then developed a verdict as to whether these beliefs were TRUE or FALSE, and wrote their verdict under the middle column on their page entitled, "VERDICT."

To decide a verdict, a person must find evidence, proof, or the truth about their situation, as best as they can determine it. As you read earlier, the book of John says that knowing the truth shall make you free (John 8:32). This truth is not just the truth of the gospel, but also the truth about your perceptions of life, love, and your spouse. Determining the truth about your partner can truly set you free.

Ephesians 4:25 says, "Therefore each of you must put off falsehood and speak truthfully to his neighbor, for we are all members of one body" (NIV). Your old brain and reactivity can create falsehoods about your spouse that can be hard to heal. They can cause you to make up realities about your partner that may not be accurate. Satan, the deceiver, can also whisper falsehoods about your spouse in your ear. The truth is what contradicts these falsehoods and creates a new and positive image of your spouse.

So how do you go about determining the truth? Here are a few ways that we recommend. This part of the exercise will require that you move into the logical, rational, left side of the brain. Under the column marked "EVIDENCE," write all the objective, observable realities that you can that you know to be true. List all the evidence you can to prove that your impression or idea is true. You may use what your partner says and does, Scripture passages, and prayer all as means of determining the truth as objectively as possible. Let's use Donna and Alex as an example to show you how the *True Vision Exercise* works.

Donna and Alex's True Vision Exercise

In her Soul Healogram, Donna saw women as responsible for keeping marriages together. Men, in turn, were distant and aloof. The conclusion she drew from this was: *Women care more than men about their marriages.* She also had a soul impression that her father was unfaithful. The false beliefs she formulated from this were: *Men cannot be faithful,* and *Alex may be unfaithful to me, as well.* Donna listed these on the far left side of a sheet of paper under the column marked "BELIEFS." She then determined whether this belief was TRUE or FALSE, and wrote her verdict after every belief she had formulated. She was responsible to find evidence to verify her verdict. She listed these things under the column marked "EVIDENCE" on the right-hand side of the page.

Alex learned from his Soul Healogram that he had developed false beliefs that women suffocated men and wanted to control things to get their way. He thought marriage was confining and took away a man's freedom. He listed these beliefs in a column on the left of his page and determined a verdict as to their validity. He then wrote realities or truths that validated his new beliefs about his marriage on the right-hand side of his paper. The following pages show an example of what Donna and Alex wrote:

Donna's True Vision Exercise

Belief	Verdict	Evidence
Men cannot be faithful.	True	In my parents' marriage.
	False	Some men find fidelity important.
Alex cannot be faithful to me.	False	Alex states that he values fidelity.
		Alex has always been faithful.
Alex is like all the men in my family and does not want to spend time with me.	False	Alex is working on goals to spend time with his family.
		Alex will go to counseling to learn how to do this.
All marriages in my family are unhappy and mine will be too.	False	Our marriage has a chance to work because we will consciously work on it.
		Alex and I demonstrate every day that our marriage is important and that working on our happiness is a priority.
		No one in my family ever did this.

Alex's True Vision Exercise

Belief	Verdict	Evidence
Women suffocate men and want control.	False	Donna says she does not want to control.
Women want their way.	True	With my mother, mostly.
	False	Donna is working on her control issues in counseling.
Marriage is confining to men.	True	In my parent's marriage.
	False	In my marriage. Although Donna desires closeness, she wants to give me freedom.
Marriage takes away a man's freedom.	False	Our marriage will add to our lives, not take away from them, because we will work hard at it in counseling.

Donna was instructed to read her "EVIDENCE" or truths several times daily, particularly when she would fear that the "Old Alex" would return. Alex was instructed to do the same. There were many more false beliefs that Donna and Alex had to correct as they became loving and willing partners to help each other. By doing this exercise, you can see how Donna and Alex had to deal with their old brainers, their negative soul impressions, and reactivity all in one blow.

It became apparent to Donna and Alex while doing this exercise that their issues impacted each other in an extremely destructive way. The problems Alex discovered as wounds for him were the very things that threw Donna into a tailspin and made her feel that Alex did not care about her. They learned that they were actually attracted to someone who had wounds that were similar to their own, but opposite adaptations. They learned that it is typical for the person with a fear of abandonment to be attracted to the person with a fear of engulfment, which creates the classic pursuer/distancer or catch-me-if-you-can couple.

Donna did not consciously know that Alex had a fear of being engulfed, or that he needed distance, but she did admire his independence, his strength, and the fact that he could stand alone so securely. Little did she know that these qualities would be carried out in their marriage through his struggle for space and freedom from her. Eventually, these independent qualities were just the characteristics that hurt Donna the most.

We see the same phenomenon with Donna's fear of abandonment and her clinging to Alex. At first he thought she was loving and affectionate, but soon he grew to resent her need for closeness and thought it was suffocating. What they both realized through learning this information was: *The fact that they can wound each other so harshly means that they have more power to heal each other.*

In fact, Alex was the most powerful person to heal Donna, and Donna was the most potent healer for Alex. This intimate enemy with whom they struggled actually held the key to their healing. Donna and Alex worked hard to catch a true vision of each other, which set them free to see themselves and each other in a more positive light. Donna began to see Alex as wounded instead of withholding, afraid instead of aloof, and hurting instead of distant. Alex, in turn, saw Donna as scared instead of demanding, hurting instead of whiny, and wounded instead of suffocating. After several months of healing, neither was tempted to put the wrong faces on their partners or make up false realities about each other again. Their extreme reactivity and negative soul impressions about each other and their marriage began to disappear. They directed their energy toward healing each other's souls, and thus became very good friends and soul healing lovers.

If you grew up in a home that contained a great deal of dysfunction, your tendency toward false beliefs about your mate will be very high. I remember when we were dating, Tom would commit some minor offense like being late to pick me up, and I would accuse him of something outrageous like never loving me. I drew a pretty harsh conclusion from such a small crime. He, on the other hand, would have a great deal of trouble seeing me as his friend if we were in conflict. The True Vision Exercise was very helpful for us to learn to see each other in a healthier, more realistic light.

Getting a true vision of your mate is priceless, but often we have couples who come to us and fear that they are hopeless from the start because they feel like all the love is gone. They, like the song says, have "lost that lovin' feelin'." If this is the case in your marriage, you may feel like it is just too hard to do these exercises. Don't give up yet. The next chapter has a wealth of information about love that will help you work through this dilemma.

CHAPTER 6

THE SOUL IN LOVE

George and Margaret had been married eighteen years and had two teenage children. They came into our counseling office because they heard us speak about falling in love on a radio talk show and they thought we could help. They were living parallel lives, and both said that they were no longer "in love." They did not want to divorce because they did not want their children to suffer, but they did not want to live in a loveless marriage, either. Their relationship had not always been so lackluster. Here is how it started.

George met Margaret at a church group. It was Margaret's first time in the group. George was sure, because he would have remembered a vision as lovely as she had she been there before. His eyes met hers, and it happened—a fleeting glance, a subtle smile of approval, and then the famous double take. It was sheer destiny that they floated toward each other, totally oblivious to everyone else in the class. Their eyes gazed and fixated upon each other. With hearts beating fast and palms sweating, they gaped in nervous silence. George had a large dry lump in his throat as he spoke, "You're new here, aren't you?"

"Why, yes, I am," Margaret replied. After the proper but somewhat awkward introductions, they never heard another word the group leader said. They were too busy listening to each other's hearts pounding.

Romantic Love

What is this wonderfully buoyant, radiant, yet anxiety-provoking feeling? What is it that causes one's heart and soul to receive a strong whollop at the sight of a prospective lover? Some call it attraction, some infatuation, some simply lust, and others romantic love.

This mystery has caused Tom and I to embark on a seemingly endless quest for what constitutes love. What is this feeling? Why do we feel it? Why do we feel it with some and not others? What is soul mating? Is falling in love real? Is there a difference between falling in love and choosing to love?

These are the questions that prompted our search for the holy grail of romance. We discovered several theories about love that were very insightful, and began to answer many of our haunting questions about relationships. By sharing these various theories with you, perhaps we all can begin to see why the heart does what it does when it is in love.

A good place to start is where romantic love started. Our culture did not always embrace the notion of falling in love. For years, marriages were arranged or transacted like business deals or property settlements. So how did our society get into this scary game of feelings and chance? In fact, I was sure that people rebelled against arranged marriages because they wanted love to be more spiritual and mystical. Perhaps westerners even wanted God to select their mate, not their parents. Unfortunately, this is not what I found as I looked at the history of romantic love.

The Origin of Romantic Love

Romantic love started around the twelfth century when the lords, or wealthy landowners, in Europe left their castles to fight the Crusades. This left their aristocratic wives alone with no one to entertain them. There were no dances or parties for them to attend. So they sat waiting for their husbands to return. This is where our society gets the term "ladies in waiting." These women had no means of entertainment—until the troubadours entered from the south of France.

The troubadours were the young (probably teenage) sons of the extremely wealthy French noblemen. Basically, they were young studs who approached the courts on beautiful horses with silk sashes. These troubadours came to the courts complete with guitars and serenaded these women with love songs. This soon became known as *courtly love*, or later *courting*.

Courtly love made the theme of male supplication and entreaty of the female popular. The troubadours would humbly petition the attention and admiration of the women in the castles. These women would select a young swain or suitor and throw a flower or a handkerchief off the tower of the castle to show their desire to claim their beau. This custom continued many centuries later in American culture.

I (Bev) grew up in the deep south. I often visit traditional southern cities like Savannah and Charleston and see the courting porches on some of the old Victorian homes there. The porches are designed for women to go to the top and throw down a handkerchief or flower to the gentleman they selected in order to identify them as a chosen suitor or beau.

My hillbilly grandmother, who died at age 104, told a story of how my grandfather would show up on the stoop of their courting porch in the cool summer evenings. This was his way of showing interest in her. She, too, was interested, so one evening she threw a hankie with her initials on it off her porch to my grandfather in order to let him know. Apparently this did the trick, because they got married shortly afterward. It was interesting for us to see that all of this was started centuries ago, from an elaborate ritual that developed between the idle noblewomen whose husbands were away in the Crusades, and their aspiring suitors.

The problem with this elaborate practice was that these young swains would have been torn to bits if there was any hint of physical connection or consummation of the relationship. In those days it was a law that a man could not even speak to a married woman, much less touch them, without fear of being put in the dungeon or getting the torture chamber or the rack. It seems that the origin of romance did not involve speaking, touching, or sex at all.

So this is the origin of our current way of mating, a fantasy relationship between forbidden would-be lovers that is full of flirtation, myth, and wanting, with virtually no basis in reality and no chance of real connection. In other words, it involves two bored people playing at a pretend relationship that has no basis in reality. More clearly, it includes bored, middle-aged, aristocratic women who have an unhealthy fantasy of wanting and longing for teenage boys who drive up in fast cars (beautifully decorated horses) and sing them love songs.

Learning the roots of romantic love was somewhat troubling for us as relationship therapists, and yet we see countless individuals who live, breathe, eat, and sleep just to get a taste of this romantic bliss. Unfortunately, it is simply a myth and a fantasy. It is no wonder that people in our culture say they are unfulfilled at love. What they are searching for has its roots in lunacy and aberration, not in solid reality, consciousness, or health.

Does this notion bother anyone else but us? We have a society that cannot sell chewing gum or toothpaste without having some steamy romantic couple in the forefront. And the origin is based on an ancient ritual of wanting and longing. Sometimes we think our society would do better with arranged marriages. Perhaps the notion that one had to stay in a marriage would stop the insipid search for the perfect lover that so consumes our society since those illustrious troubadours in the twelfth century. In fact, we actually entertained the idea of changing our research and the focus of this book and writing *Why Westerners Should Move to Arranged Marriages*, but we were sure that publishers would not be interested. Besides, there are 147 other cultures that have joined us in making romantic love a major means of mate selection.[1]

As you can see, Tom and I are not alone in our societal dilemma. Since we cannot change the modern method of mate selection in our society, or in any other culture for that matter, we are left to work with what we have. The goal, then, is to understand romantic love and make it more healthy and conscious for those who wish to drink from its well. We want to help those mystical would-be lovers learn all that they can about the theories of romantic love.

The Theory of Eros

The first theory of romantic love is that of *Eros*. Many in western civilization think *Eros* is the burning ember of passion between a man and a woman. *Eros* is sensual and sexual in nature, and therefore a key piece of this theory of romance is physical and sexual attraction. Another name for it could even be lust. When you see someone across the room and you find yourself strongly attracted to them, *Eros* or its more lustful properties are operating. You may meet someone that just looks like "your type," with certain physical characteristics, coloring, style, movements, gestures, and posturings that create desire and make you want to get close to that person. This is *Eros* at work.

Author Dr. Neil Warren, in his book *Finding the Love of Your Life*, states that many relational psychologists feel that building a deeper relationship is impossible without the physical attraction and excitement that come from passionate love. He sees this passionate love (or *Eros*) between two people as a critical ingredient if they are to have a long, satisfying relationship.[2] While *Eros* is important in the mating process, many people in our society make it the primary litmus-paper test for true love, and negate other very significant mating factors. Thus, when attraction fades and passionate love wanes, the commitment is in danger of fading, as well.

We, as relationship therapists, have found *Eros* to be a very misunderstood concept. The Greeks knew *Eros* had its sensual and sexual qualities, but the true meaning of the word is only sexual in part. In the original Greek, the word *Eros* is defined as life breath or life energy. This is a far cry from basic passionate love, or fleshly lust. Yet in our workshops we ask people what they think of when we use the term *Eros,* and most of them say things like "erotic," "sexy," "sleazy," and "pornographic." The images brought to mind are seedy and perverse. The Greeks knew that people needed to feel life force or life energy. They found it in many forms, not just sex. Literature, poetry, sports, building, talking, sharing, and simply creating were ways for them to express their *Eros.*

Westerners have reduced *Eros* to what most people do to play as adults—have sex. They have sexualized their life energy and think of finding their *Eros* in sexual fantasy, which usually suggests ilicit sexual bliss. There is a subtle attitude in our culture that for truly exciting fantasy-like sex to take place, it cannot happen in a relationship with one's own committed lifetime partner.

We see *Eros* in another light. We view it more from the avenue of soul, and not just the physical self. Because of this, it need not be diluted or perverted as it has been for so long in our culture. Mating and lovemaking need to be done with the soul, as well as with the body. Sexual intimacy is a sacred ritual that touches the heart of God as He blesses the lives of His children. Sex, then, is a sacred soul gift. When we view sex in this way, then *Eros* is less sexualized and can truly represent life energy or life force in humans. The goal of marriage is to provide that life energy to yourself and your mate. This would be done through learning about the soul and becoming committed to doing the things that would bring healing to it. The process of mating is a soulful process. Lovemaking is an act of soulfulness between a man and a woman, replicating our own closeness to the Lord.

Yes, sensual *Eros* and physical attraction are important in the mating process, but in learning how to truly love the soul of your mate and allowing them to love yours, they need to take a back seat to other more spiritual, soulful aspects of partnering.

The Dreamed-About Love

As we continue our study of romantic love, we find that early in our life we formulate a vision of our "ideal mate." This vision involves physical characteristics, body shape, facial appearance, smell, skin texture, hair color, and certain personality traits. We then search for this "ideal mate," hoping to find a match. Sometimes this is done with physical appearance alone, but sometimes with a touch or a kiss. Romeo and Juliet represent this type of love-at-first-sight encounter. Dr. Neil Warren says that this "dreamed-about love" enhances our self-esteem, partially because their love makes us feel good about ourselves, and partially because we feel connected to someone else.[3]

It is because of this preexisting image of our prospective mate that we pick certain people and leave others behind. While it is true that people have a mental grid that includes whom they may be attracted to, this apparition of the "dreamed-about love" is not all that there is in the mating process. This leads us to another theory of mating called the *Imago*.

The Theory of Imago

Dr. Harville Hendrix has done groundbreaking work in the development of Imago Relationship Theory. *Imago* is a Latin term meaning "image" or "image of." Dr. Hendrix believes that we are attracted to the unconscious image of the negative and positive traits of our primary caretakers. He calls this image our *Imago*. The theory espouses that we are unconsciously attracted to these negative traits in order to get prospective mates to embody the positive traits of our primary caretakers. Thus we can "create" the positive caretakers we want so desperately. All of this is extremely unconscious, but it explains why we see so many people pick mates who replicate characteristics in their family of origin that defy logic. An example might be the daughter of an abusive alcoholic who unconsciously selects an alcoholic husband. This woman may vow that she will never marry a man like her father. She may even look for a prospective husband at Al Anon meetings in hopes of finding a man who does not drink, but she still is high risk for picking a partner who has some form of addiction.

Imago Theory has as one of its premises the old Freudian notion of "repetition compulsion." This is the tendency to repeat patterns in life that are familiar to our unconscious memory. In other words, we are not fully aware of our hidden need to relive that which is familiar and comfortable. The *Imago* serves as an unconscious homing device that causes us to be attracted to those individuals who enable us to repeat patterns in our childhood and perhaps "get them right" this time. We are attracted to a person who can heal our childhood wounds and give us the love we have always wanted. This explains why when we fall in love, we feel a familiarity and a comfort around our loved one that has a mystical quality. The feeling that "I have known you all my life" is part of our unconscious homing instinct that helps heal our woundedness. This soulful desire for healing is the driving force behind the relationship.[4]

Another premise of Imago Theory is that we are attracted to individuals who have complimentary adaptations to the socialization process. In simpler terms, this means that we are attracted to individuals who have similar wounds, but different ways of dealing with them. We become paired with incompatible partners in order to create chemistry for growth. We are attracted to what is missing or lost in ourselves. The shy boy will be extremely attracted the social butterfly. Being with her makes him feel more socially adept. Thus his woundedness can be healed in her presence. The easily embarrassed female who has trouble showing affection in public meets the handsome guy who is free with his public displays of affection, and she feels a stimulation that she has never felt before. Hendrix quotes:

Chances are that the people you are drawn to and admire possess qualities that you long for, or that were dismissed and disdained in your home. If you get close to such people, you feel good about yourself, more complete, through association. In the presence of our opposites, we can retrieve our missing parts and feel whole.[5]

I (Bev) must admit, I was skeptical of this theory at first, thinking that my husband was nothing like my extremely dysfunctional caretakers. With further exploration and some training in Dr. Hendrix's work, I was stunned to see there was a huge correlation between the characteristics of my family of origin and my mate. I was equally surprised when I saw that I could replicate many of the negative characteristics of my in-laws. Thank goodness I have quite a few of their positive characteristics as well.

I also noticed that Tom possessed some of the lost or missing parts of me. When I met Tom, I was nonassertive and passive. I apologized to everyone for everything. On our first date, I was upset because my steak was so rare it was pink and I could not eat it. I was much too embarrassed to send it back—but not Tom.

"Waiter," he called in his most assertive voice. "Send this steak back and have the chef cook it more. My girl can't eat pink meat."

Wow, what a hero, I thought. He could confront a rude salesperson or get his order right. Now that's something that was missing in me. When I was with him, I felt protected, whole, and complete. He was the embodiment of my opposite. He had characteristics that I was lacking.

On the other hand, I was very merciful and would give money away to various mission and charitable organizations. Tom admired this, because he had a natural built-in skepticism for many support-funded organizations. This came from a wound he had suffered when the church was not there for him during his parent's divorce. Being with me helped him feel more trusting and philanthropic. He felt complete in my presence, as if that part of him was redeemed.

The downside of the *Imago* is that while the potential partner is seen as the glorious healer of our childhood wounds, they also possess the characteristics that could deeply wound our souls. Imagine that the person who has the greatest power to bring healing to your soul has the same power to murder your soul, as well. Because of this, enraptured lovers can become bitter enemies. In fact, we have noticed that the degree of bitterness a couple feels after a breakup is directly proportional to the degree of love or need that they once felt in the relationship. This power to wound one's partner is what marital contempt is made of.

Tom and I have seen this resentful contempt firsthand with our own parents' divorces. Tom's parents were married twenty-six years. Together they created two talented, bright, attractive children. They had twenty-six Christmases, twenty-six vacations, and a great many memories. At one point, they were partners, lovers, and friends, yet now they are bitter enemies. The same is true for my parents. Even after four children and eleven years as a married couple, they do not speak to each other. It baffles us as to how they can love someone enough to marry them, have children with them, and share the most intimate of life experiences with them, only to relegate them to the vitriolic position of caustic archenemy. We are amazed at how the line between love and hate is so tentative. The same positive energy of *Imago's* bonding power can acidify and poison a marriage.

Dr. Hendrix's theory of the conscious relationship is designed to solve this problem. He believes that becoming aware of the woundedness in yourself and your spouse can help you become better, more conscious marriage partners. As you become aware of your mate's hurts and pains, hopefully you will be less likely to harm him or her in these areas. Preventing couples from re-injuring old childhood wounds goes a long way toward healing.

The Theory of Chemistry, or Limerance

While to this point we have evaluated our erotic mating rituals and looked at our *Imago*, it is now time to evaluate what part chemistry plays in relationships. What is chemistry anyway? We all know what we think it is. It's that giddy feeling we get when we see a certain someone. We feel weak-kneed, breathless, and often times shaky. We do a double take, and are compelled to get just one more glance or ask one more inane question. The feeling that pulsates throughout our bodies is known as *chemistry*. The term *chemistry* has its roots in *alchemy*, a form of science and philosophy made popular in the Middle Ages when alchemists were attempting to discover an elixir for life. Alchemists philosophized about the seemingly magical process that transformed ordinary materials into something of true merit. The term *chemistry* was coined to describe two common ordinary humans interacting with such energy that there was true merit in their encounter, or more accurately, true love. Author Dorothy Tennov, in her book *Love and Limerance*, calls this blissful state of feeling like you can walk on air *limerance*. She refers to limerance as…

> …*the sense that one has found the key to happiness in the presence of their partner. There is an acute longing for reunification, an aching in the chest, followed by obsessive and intrusive thoughts about the loved one. There is an initial attraction and excitement that causes one to see his or her partner as utterly wonderful.*[6]

These feelings of chemistry, or limerance, can also be described less mystically as a simple sympathetic understanding, harmonious interaction, or a solid rapport, thus explaining statements like these: "My new love can finish my sentences," "He seems to know what I am thinking," "We are like two musical instruments playing in intimate harmony," "I feel understood by her," and "I have told him things I have never shared with anyone." These are the illustrious manifestations of chemistry.

Chemistry, however, is not all it is acclaimed to be. It can be very unhealthy for some people. If you had unhealthy parents who did not treat you fairly, then you may also pick an unhealthy mate. This is why some people only have chemistry for "losers," whom they can fix. We once had a client who realized that she only had chemistry for men who needed her. Consequently, she kept picking men who were irresponsible and dependent, much like her mother. When she would meet a man who was very giving and interested in her, she found him boring, and would be disappointed because there was no spark.

While some chemistry is necessary for a relationship to grow, it needs to be examined to determine whether or not it is healthy. If you find that you are attracted to a certain "type," and that "type" is always hurting you, you may need to alter the amount of chemistry you deem necessary in order to feel the relationship can grow deeper. The following story illustrates this.

Jan's Story

Jan came to our office because her fiancé had broken off their engagement one month before the wedding. She was severely depressed and suicidal.

"I have nothing to live for," she cried. "Michael was my whole life. After three years, he decided that he didn't have what it took to be married to me. I guess I was just too hard to love."

Michael was not the first man to leave Jan. She described a series of relationships in which she was strongly attracted to men who were distant, aloof, and critical. She and her girlfriends had a saying that "nice guys are a dime a dozen." In other words, if he wasn't a challenge, she did not want to pursue him.

While exploring Jan's background, it came as no surprise to us that her father was an alcoholic. She was the oldest of four children whom she cared for when her father was drunk. She described her father as handsome, energetic, and fun—when he was sober. But when he would drink, he would withdraw and become moody, sullen, and critical. As the oldest child, Jan felt responsible to pull him out of his withdrawal. She would love to make him laugh when he was drinking, in hopes that he would interact more with the family and not be so sullen. Jan learned early to associate chemistry and attraction with getting a seemingly distant man to pay positive attention to her.

As you can see, she was playing out the same dynamics from her interaction with dad in her adult dating relationships. She was caught in a repetition compulsion from her childhood. Thus she unconsciously selected men with whom she would have to replay the same childhood struggles. There was tremendous chemistry with these men, but they were deadly for her self-esteem, not to mention that they never truly committed to her.

In counseling, Jan learned to see that she needed to consciously select men who were more loving, and much less challenging. This would mean that she would probably have to settle for less chemistry. There would still be an attraction, but her encounters would not pack as much punch. At first this was hard for her, but what kept her trying was the lingering pain she felt after each breakup.

Eventually Jan felt comfortable with a more moderate level of chemistry; that was when she met Bobby. He was much more introverted than her previous beaus, but also much more emotionally and physically available. Once Jan got past the "nice guy" phenomenon, she found that Bobby was quite interesting. Her feeling that nice guys were boring, or "a dime a dozen," began to fade. It was great to see Jan start to feel at ease with being loved and cared for. She learned that she no longer had to play out the struggles of her childhood. To make a long story short, Jan and Bobby were married and committed to being soul healers for a lifetime. Jan will be the first to tell you that chemistry can be very misleading in the mating process.

One of the biggest problems with chemistry is that it fades. Just ask anyone who has been married for a while. We have even noticed this in our own marriage. The newness wears off, and some of the thrill passes. No longer do you wait for your spouse with bated breath. You don't get as tingly when he or she enters the room. Because chemistry tends to decline or weaken, many relational theorists are stressing that less emphasis be placed on the feelings of being "in love," and more emphasis placed on the conscious decision to love one's partner. They focus on the fact that love is more of a choice than a feeling, and thus emotions should play a more secondary role in the mating process.

As we begin to examine what part chemistry should play in mate selection, it would be valuable to look at some recent research in the field of neurobiology that shows that there is a biological link between our heads and our hearts, especially where chemistry is concerned. In fact, after we did this research, we changed the term "falling in love" to "tripping into infatuation," because the fall is more like a stumble and the love is not real love at all.

The Biology of Love

Have you ever wondered why you have such strong physiological triggers when you fall in love with someone? What makes your heart pound? Why do you feel butterflies in your stomach? The feeling that you can walk on air, the lack of need for food or sleep, the superhuman feeling that comes with more adrenalin, these are all physical signs of "love." Why do these manifestations occur? Some people believe that the occurrence of these phenomena is a sure sign that true love is present. I once believed this myself, but recent developments in neurobiology may show us differently.

The Love Cocktail

Research shows that when a person falls in love, or trips into infatuation, his or her brain is flooded with chemicals. These include norepinephrine, epinephrine, dopamine, and especially phenylethylamine, PEA for short. These chemicals make up what Michael Liebowitz, from the New York State Psychiatric Institute, calls "the love cocktail."[7] Symptoms from these neurotransmitters working in concert are: a delightful positive attitude, increased energy and a decreased need for sleep, loss of appetite, and general euphoria. Wow, who wouldn't want a hit of that!? It causes you to feel superhuman. A meeting of eyes, a touch of hands, or a whiff of a scent sets off a flood that starts in the brain and races along the nerves and through the bloodstream. The results are familiar: flushed skin, sweaty palms, and heavy breathing. Above all, there is the sheer euphoria of falling in love. This explains why we have such an altered physical state when we fall in love. It also helps us put the notion of falling in love into a more clear and rational perspective.

Now that we know that the love cocktail will blast through our systems when we are in the presence of someone who could be a potential partner, we can consciously and sanely decide whether we want to pursue this relationship or not. We no longer have to assume that our biological triggers should dictate who our lifetime partners will be. We also do not have to overlook those potential partners who do not cause the whistle to blow as hard in the PEA factory. We no longer have to be a slave to our biological signals when it comes to love.

This is good news for this generation of would-be partners, because further research suggests that brain-chemical highs, laced with phenylethylamine, do not last. Like any other chemical, the body begins to develop a tolerance to it. It then takes more and more of the substance to produce love's special kick. After four years, the body simply can't crank the needed amount of the love cocktail. This makes passionate romantic love short-lived. Fizzling chemicals spell the end of delirious passion. For many people, this marks the end of the relationship, as well. This is especially true for what is known as "attraction junkies." They crave the intoxication of falling in love so much that they move frantically from relationship to relationship just as soon as the first rush of infatuation fades.

In premarital counseling sessions, we ask couples what their worst fear is. So many times they say they are worried that the wonderful, giddy feeling of being in love will fade. We now know that not only will it fade, but that it is a biological necessity. Like any other chemical, the body builds up a tolerance to PEA, and it simply cannot crank enough of it to produce the sizzle it once did. Besides, the constant flow of these natural amphetamines places a great deal of stress on the body. When we fall in love, our neurological system is stressed. The body cannot take this kind of stress indefinitely. This feeling needs to fade, not only to give our bodies a break, but also to make room for real, sane, conscious, willful, soul healing love.

Here is some great news that we found. Biology also gives us a reward for long-term committed love. The brain's pituitary gland secretes endorphins that are natural painkillers. These give lovers a sense of security, peace, and calm. This is the reason why we feel so horrible when a partner dies. We do not have our daily hit of narcotics. Oxytocin is a chemical that is released many times when long-term couples make love. Many scientists call it the "cuddle chemical." It gives couples a sensation that all is right with the world. So, you see, if you hang on after the phenylethylamine has faded, you will get the chance to take advantage of one of nature's other more soothing remedies. Commitment does have its rewards.

The last theory of romantic love is perhaps the most complex. While it may be difficult to grasp at first, it offers some excellent information on love that may be helpful to you.

The Theory of Projection

The Theory of Projection has its inception in the premise that we carry in each of our souls both masculine and feminine characteristics. This has important implications for the relationship between the sexes. Men typically project their feminine side onto women to whom they are attracted, and women typically project their masculine side onto men they are attracted to. Wherever projection occurs, the person who carries the projected image is extremely overvalued. The real, true person is greatly obscured by the projected image. In other words, females who have not embraced their masculine characteristics may put these onto men who are possible mates. Likewise, men who have not embraced their feminine side may project this onto women. The person who carries this projected psychic image of another has a great deal of power over them. As long as a part of a person's psyche is perceived in someone else, that person has some form of control over the perceiver. At first the prospective partner may feel valued and flattered to be seen in such a positive light. They are willing to identify themselves with the powerful images that are projected upon them because it is an escape from the more humble task of recognizing their true personalities.

When a woman projects her positive masculine side onto a man, she may have a delusional image of him as savior, hero, and spiritual guide, all rolled into one. She overvalues him, is fascinated by him, and is mystically drawn to him. He is seen by her as the ultimate man or the ideal lover. She is completed only through him, she is whole only in his presence, what is lost is now found. Through him, she has found her soul mate. She is content to be a loving moth around his flame. What she is not seeing, however, is that she has abandoned her search for the positive masculine qualities within herself. She has displaced them on to her ideal man and therefore does not have to find them or refine them within herself. Unfortunately, her quest for the perfect love may just shortcut her own personal growth.

Because this feeling of love is based purely on projections, this state of being in love is delusional and not based on reality. People fall in love with an image, not a real person. Dr. John Sanford, in his book *Invisible Partners*, says that…,

> …*relationships founded exclusively on the being-in-love state can never last…. The inability of the state of being in love to endure the stress of everyday life is recognized by all great poets. This is why Romeo and Juliet had to end in death. It would have been unthinkable for Shakespeare to have concluded his great love story by*

sending his loving couple to Sears to buy pans for the kitchen. They would have quarreled in an instant over what frying pan to choose and how much it was going to cost, and the whole beautiful story would have evaporated.[8]

In Summary

To summarize all these theories of romantic love, we see that we can pick a partner on the basis of attraction, chemistry, limerance, phenylethylamine (PEA), our *Imago*, our dreamed-about mate, or our projections. All of this has taught us that falling in love is not a rational or conscious process, and it is not based in reality. You saw that falling in love and out of love is more "insane" than we think. Therefore, we are left with one conclusion: True, soul healing love is a sane, rational, conscious process of choice. It involves an act of the will, not just of the heart. Soul healing love is a commitment of the soul that is more of a decision than flighty feelings. It is hard work, but it is indeed worth it. The next chapter is committed to showing you how to do this difficult, yet fulfilling, work.

CHAPTER 7

MAKING LOVE WORK

*M*ary and Lou had been married for fourteen years. They had the American dream: two kids, two cars, a big house complete with a big mortgage, and a successful business that kept them both very busy. Mary called our office because she wanted Christian marriage counseling. It seemed that several years before, their good friends, Rick and Amber, were on the verge of divorce and had come to see us. They attended a Soul Healers Workshop and began to mend their marriage.

Mary felt their marriage needed a facelift, and Lou reluctantly agreed. In the first session, it was obvious that Mary was the expressive, emotional part of this duo. She did most of the talking, and Lou would nod and respond in a logical, matter-of-fact manner. Both described their marriage as sagging. They shared that they were distant from each other and their communication was stilted.

Their family history revealed that Mary was the oldest of two children. Her younger brother, Murray, was a very rebellious teenager who had become a drug addict during his adolescence. He would be what we call in family therapy the "identified patient." She stated that Murray still caused the family grief by continuing to live his life in a very unhealthy manner. He typically drifted from job to job and continued a drug habit that started in his youth. Mary played the role of caretaker for her younger brother, which established codependent patterns very early in her life. She also played the role of "family hero" taking responsibility for upholding the good name of the family. While Murray was tearing the family down by playing the bad kid, Mary was responsible for building it up by playing the good kid. She made straight As, was the drum majorette of the band and president of the honor society, and was an all around exemplary child. Her mother's favorite statement to her was, "You have never given me a minute's worth of trouble," and the implied message was, "You must be good at all costs." Performing for love and acceptance became a way of life for Mary.

Lou, Mary's husband, was the youngest of four boys. He grew up in Philadelphia in a rough neighborhood and got into trouble early in life. He quit school when he was sixteen and ran the streets. He drank and used drugs regularly. After a brush with the law, his father convinced him to join the army to get some "discipline." In the military, he finished high school and earned a college education. When he left the army, he landed a great job in a high-pressure sales firm. Because he was a natural salesman, he went straight to the top. He was making great money, and things were finally going his way.

It was at this time that he met Mary. It was love at first sight. They couldn't get enough of each other. He wined and dined her at the finest restaurants. They traveled to exotic places. He even took her to Vail, Colorado for two weeks and patiently taught her how to ski. They had a whirlwind romance. On the chemistry scale of one to ten, they said they were an eleven. We shared with them about brain chemicals such as phenylethylamine being released when a person falls in love, and both agreed that their (PEA) levels were significantly high.

Mary remembered seeing some hints of Lou's irresponsibility while they dated. There were times when he would not go into the office and failed to return phone calls from clients, but she chalked this up to his being in love and wanting to spend all the time with her that he could. Lou would get back on track and settle down after they were married. Mary was sure of it. In six months they were married. Mary had plans of settling down and establishing more of a routine. Lou still wanted to travel and play.

"We can't afford to keep up this lifestyle," she would plead. "We need to save money for our future."

"Let's live for the moment. We have plenty of time to settle down. Don't be such a party pooper," Lou would reply.

And so the honeymoon was over and the power struggle started, with Mary wanting to establish a more conservative lifestyle and Lou wanting to live unencumbered. Gradually they began to drift apart.

After about four years, Mary felt the magic and chemistry start to fade. She feared that maybe she had made a mistake. Maybe she had married the wrong man. She kept this fear deep inside and, being the over-responsible person she was, decided to do everything she could to make her marriage work. Very soon she got pregnant, and William, their son, was born. She now had something to consume her time and interest. She loved being a mother, and Will's birth seemed to bring her and Lou closer. Pouring herself into parenting Will became her main focus. She did not want him to turn out like her brother, Murray. She was determined not to make her parent's mistakes. Lou began to feel more and more neglected. He started hanging out after work with some fellow sales reps at a local pub. Before he knew it, Lou was drinking every night and excessively on the weekends. Mary noticed this, but when she confronted Lou, he became defensive and denied that he had a problem. He told her that if she would pay more attention to him when he was home, then maybe he wouldn't stay out with his friends.

Finally, Lou stopped coming home at all on Friday nights. This went on for several months, and one Saturday Mary got a concerned phone call from Lou's boss. He told Mary that Lou's work was slipping, and his attendance was poor. He suspected that Lou had a drug problem. When Lou finally came home that weekend, Mary confronted him. After a huge argument, he reluctantly admitted that he had been using cocaine, and it was becoming a real problem for him.

In shock, Mary threatened to leave if he did not get help. So Lou checked himself into a local Christian treatment center. He had an experience with God and started to sober up. Things began to improve in their lives and in their marriage. They joined a local church and became very active there. It was about this time that Lou started his own business. Mary soon got pregnant with their second child, a girl. They had their family, their faith, and their health. What more could they ask for? But deep inside of Mary, there was still a nagging feeling that something was missing in her marriage. When their minister preached on spiritual oneness in a marital relationship, she would come home longing and depressed.

Lou's business consumed a great deal of his time, and he pressured Mary to work for him. This had been a pattern in their relationship in the past. They had many arguments about it that eventually precipitated her call for counseling. It seemed that after her daughter's birth, she no longer had the drive or the stamina to work in Lou's business. It reminded her too much of the days when she was his caretaker. She wanted to devote all of her attention to being a full-time mom. Lou resented this because he felt unsupported and abandoned. He was frustrated because he said that Mary nagged him to come home all the time, and if she would help him in the business, he could come home more. Mary was upset because she did not want the pressure of taking care of him any longer. She wanted him to stand on his own two feet. The more she would nag, the more he would distance. Thus we could see the typical pattern of the pursuer/distancer played out in their relationship. They, like many of the other couples in therapy, were playing "marital Pac-Man" where one mate pursues and the other runs from them for fear of being "chomped up."

In their marriage counseling sessions, Tom and I told Mary and Lou that marriages go through stages similar to the way children go through stages in their development.[1] Sharing these stages with couples seems to validate and normalize their frustrated feelings about marriage, and establishes a foundation for healing.

The Stages of Marriage

So many couples do not know what to expect in matrimony. Since they have no idea what is coming next, they feel a sense of panic or even doom when the relationship shifts or changes. Every human experience has three basic phases, and marriage is no different. The beginning phase of any experience is the *Expansion Stage*. During this time, one is apt to feel hopeful and filled with positive expectations.

What usually comes after any new experience? *Disillusionment.* Yes, disappointment comes because some things do not work out the way you thought. The new job was not the answer to your problems. The college education did not yield the perfect career. Marriage has its own set of disappointments, yet society puts so much pressure on couples to feel positive all of the time. Any hint of disillusionment in matrimony causes you to feel like the magic has faded, or you have made the wrong choice. We, as marriage counselors, contend that you need to *expect* disappointment in marriage. Anticipate it, and then when it happens, you will not be so shocked, and you will also be strong enough to handle it.

The last stage of all human experience is *Resolution*. This comes only through accepting your current state of disillusionment and doing what you can to make a difference. The problem with marriage is that many times couples become so disheartened that their only form of resolution is the dissolution of their marriage. We have seen that making couples aware of the stages of marriage is very beneficial in helping them normalize their fear and panic about their struggles, and then reach resolution about their marital frustrations and disappointments. The stages of marriage are as follows.

Stage 1: Romantic Love

The first stage of a love relationship is that of *Romantic Love*. As you saw in the previous chapter, this stage is characterized by positive brain chemicals and delusion. During this delusional stage, we believe our partner to be our hero, or the answer to all our problems. At this time our "chosen one" can do no wrong. I once had a client tell me that when her new boyfriend cleared up his bankruptcy, ended his probation for beating his ex-wife, and got his children back from social services, that everything was going to be wonderful in their lives. Was she delusional or what? One of our workshop attendees put it best when she said, "When I first met my husband, I thought he was perfect, but now I know that my brain was just on drugs."

You learned earlier that the romantic love stage is not based on reality. It is highly emotional and full of positive projections. During this time you want to see your partner all the time. You just can't seem to get enough of him or her. This is partially because the love cocktail is activated in the presence of your partner, and partly because you feel so secure when you are with them. Couples spend the whole day with each other, and then go home and immediately call each other. They use pet names and talk "baby talk" to one another. Their interaction looks much like a mother bonding with her newborn infant. Couples use this time to bond and form an attachment, as well. As couples settle into reality, their interactions become more and more routine. Warts and scars on their precious partners that went previously undetected now loom ominously on the horizon. These disheartened couples find that they are enter-ing into what Harville Hendrix calls the *Power Struggle*.[2]

Stage 2: The Power Struggle

This is the stage when our true love begins to let us down. We are counting on him to be our "knight in shining armor," or her to be a "devoted moth around our flame" who will save us from all of life's ills. One can see why we are furious when he or she turns out to be a mere mortal. Unfortunately, the Power Struggle is just as delusional as the Romantic Love Stage, but now, instead of projecting all the positive characteristics onto our mate, we give him or her all the negative ones. We are sure that our mate knows what to do to love us and meet our needs, since he or she so readily and willingly did this in the romantic stage. We now feel that he or she just stubbornly refuses to meet them. There is no fury too great for this crime. We once thought the world of our partner, but now we are arguing over toothpaste, budgets, and how many times we have made love in the last month.

Because our true love has now betrayed us, we have rancor and malice for this "villain." The sad truth is that he is no more a "villain" than he is a "knight in shining armor." We are both merely human, and now we are faced with the responsibility of seeing each other as we really are. It is hard for our soul to make sense out of the sudden change in our partner, so we make up our own realities about him or her. We assign evil or negative motives to them in order to explain their unexplainable behaviors and actions toward us. We falsely accuse our mates of intentions they do not possess and crimes they have not committed. By doing this, we overreact, or become reactive, to the offenses committed against us.

In the Soul Healing Love Model we have a working definition of a power struggle: *a relationship in which there is an underlying tension that is always there, that is characterized by fear that leads to a breakdown in communication, which leads to assumption. And in the power struggle, couples typically assume the worst and project it onto their partner.*[3]

Our couple, Mary and Lou, found themselves in a very difficult power struggle. Mary assumed the worst about Lou, and "made up" that he was just like her drug-addicted brother and would always be irresponsible. Any time Lou did anything that was the slightest bit irresponsible, she panicked and accused him of sabotaging his success. Lou was also reactive, and "made up" that Mary was a "control freak" who liked to complain because it gave her a sense of power, just like his mother. Mary would nag, blame, and coerce him into hearing her point. This hit Lou's childhood wound of being a bad boy. Mary's behavior reminded him of his mother and how she would scream at him and plead with him to stay out of trouble. Lou felt he could not do anything good enough for Mary, just like he felt with his mother. He was often passive-aggressive with Mary, promising her he would do something and then "forgetting" to do it. This would hit her wound of not feeling valued unless she was performing or caretaking, and she would retaliate in anger.

Once again, as in previous case examples, we see interactivity rear its ugly head. Mary and Lou's wounds were interactive. They were constantly making impact statements that drove the knife even further into each other's wounds. Remember, impact statements are statements made by couples out of their own woundedness that directly affect the woundedness of their spouse. These impact statements would activate Mary and Lou's old brain feelings of rejection and pain, and would cause even more hurt and destruction in their relationship.

It was obvious that Mary and Lou were not friends. They no longer saw each other as allies. In the Power Struggle stage, they became adversarial. *Eros* had turned sour, and even friendship, or *philia*, was not an option. Unfortunately, the Power Struggle stage is where most couples stay. Mary and Lou had been in it for fourteen years. They argued, fought, manipulated, and made deals. The agenda for each was to have their own way. The "I-will-die for-you" courtship had turned into a "me-first" war zone.

There is a way out of the Power Struggle, however. It is committing to become soul healers. Becoming a soul healer takes hard work. With effort and determination, a couple can move to the next stage of marriage, which is called *Awareness*.

Stage 3: The Awareness Stage

During the stage of Awareness, we come to know ourselves and each other for who we really are. We move from placing blame to seeing what part we play in our marital problems. We stop pointing fingers and start owning our woundedness. We ask ourselves a very important question: *What is it like living with ME?* The focus then is turned away from our mate's warts and flaws to our own. This is not a martyr-like attempt at self-blame or false humility, but rather an honest and courageous attempt, with the Lord's help, to see the character flaws and negative behaviors we play out in our marriage. I (Bev) remember having to answer this difficult question in my own marriage to Tom. I hate to admit it but at this time in our marriage, I was afflicted with a serious relational malady that I have since then named *Sanctimonious Christian Woman Syndrome*.

I actually thought that I was wonderful to live with. I took care of everyone in my family of origin and tried to get everything right and be as good and perfect as I could be. Therefore, the problems in our marriage *must* be Tom's. As unhealthy as it sounds, that was what I thought. I worked hard to answer the question properly in order to prove to Tom that I was blameless in our power struggle. We gave each other permission to interview people we lived with growing up to see what insights they could give us. I piously ran off to do my assignment with my interviewees in mind. First, I called my twin sister. She was my roommate for eighteen years and one of my closest friends; surely she would be a good judge of what a wonderful person I was. Her testimony would surely shine the light on my angelic qualities and thus point to the devilish Tom as the real culprit in our struggles.

I phoned her and told her that I was doing a project on what it was like living with me and that I would like her to give me some information. "Why, living with you was great!" she eagerly volunteered. "You were generous, compassionate, caring, a good listener, and a great friend."

"Hey, this is going great," I thought pridefully. "This will really make my case."

As my sister continued, I really started feeling puffed up. "You are deeply spiritual, kindhearted, and hard-working," she went on. "Now, do I get to tell you about how controlling you were?"

"Well," I harrumphed, "I think I need to go now." I ended the call in a bit of a huff. The mere idea that she would say such a thing! My case against Tom was diminishing right before my eyes.

I knew what I had to do then. I had to find another supporter to help build my argument. I would interview my younger brother. He would support my defense; after all, I had practically raised him. He would be my ally. I called him, and asked the key question—What was it like living with me?

"Oh," he said, "you were generous and kind."

"Good, good," I thought to myself. "This is working."

"Continue," I said encouragingly.

"You were always very thoughtful, and I could wake you up at two A.M. to cook me grits and gravy and you would do it."

"This is going nicely," I pridefully pondered.

He continued, "When do I get to comment about how bossy you were?"

Well, that was it! "Thank you very much," I stated in the most martyrish tone I could muster. "I'll have to talk to you later." I was truly beside myself. These evaluations were biased and skewed. "That's it," I thought to myself. "They are bogus. They must be. I'm a wonderful person with wonderful motives. I only bossed and controlled because they needed it. They were better off because of it, right?"

Boy, was I deluded! I thought that because my motives were benevolent and that I was trying to take care of everybody and everything, that my controlling behavior was okay. But it wasn't. The people in my environment did see the good that I tried to do, but they also struggled with the unhealthy way in which I did it. My points were lucid, logical, and often biblical. I could win a debate, but I would not look realistically at the part I played, and I blamed everyone, especially Tom, for our marital struggles.

To finish our assignment, we had to report our findings to each other and discuss what we had discovered from our friends and relatives about what it was like living with us. As I started to share my findings with Tom, I knew that I needed to be truthful, but my pride got in the way. I willingly and eagerly shared all the positives. "I'm generous, compassionate, a good friend, a good helper, kind-hearted, and caring." I really wanted to stop right there. That sounded so nice, but I knew that I needed to confess *all* of my findings. So, in a mumbled low tone, much like a used car salesman who practically whispers the price of a car as he shares all its attributes, I managed to quickly and quietly quip, "Oh, and by the way, I'm a little bossy and controlling."

"What?" Tom questioned, with a gleam in his eye. "I didn't hear those last two. Could you say them again, a little slower and a little louder?" I had been caught and I knew it. I had to eat crow and I didn't like it. I managed to muster the courage that humility requires and grunted, "My siblings say that I am bossy and a little controlling." At that moment, the moment of confession, I saw myself. For the first time in our marriage, I did not defend my good intentions. I did not protect my noble motives. I just confessed the truth. In doing this, I saw what it was really like living with me.

Oh, I was generous and all the rest, *but*, and this was a big *but*, I was indeed bossy and controlling. For years, Tom had tried to tell me that I was hard to live with because of this. But I would justify and rationalize my position. My Sanctimonious Christian Woman Syndrome just would not let me see my mistakes. For the first time, I saw them glaring back at me, and I was truly humbled. This humility was the beginning of my Awareness.

During our Awareness Stage, we gather information about ourselves and our mates. This is where the Soul Healogram (see Chapter Four) can be very helpful. It provides couples with a wealth of knowledge that can prove to be very beneficial in soul healing. Mary and Lou completed the Soul Healogram and found out several things that they had not known before.

Hearing about each other's woundedness was new to them and made them feel very anxious and disoriented. This is common for couples because they are giving up their old ways of behaving. They are now forced away from the "blame game," are prevented from dancing to the "you-don't-love-me" shuffle, and are propelled toward change. This change can be very scary for couples. We tell them that it gets worse before it gets better, because these new insights and behaviors are uncomfortable for them. This discomfort causes anxiety and even fear.

After Mary and Lou completed their Soul Healogram, they were ready to formulate their Soul Healing Plan. They were to write the goals for this plan independently of each other, and then share them in therapy. Their goals are listed below.

Mary's Soul Healing Plan Date: 2-14-2005

1. *That Lou and I would become soul mates and share our deep feelings with each other.*
2. That Lou would take the financial responsibility for the family.
3. That I devote full-time to caring for the children and not feel guilty about not working in the business.
4. That Lou would come home from work at a reasonable hour and spend at least one night a week having family time with the kids.
5. That we would learn to communicate better and learn to resolve conflict in a healthy manner.

Lou's Soul Healing Plan Date: 2-14-2005

1. *That Mary would stop nagging me about every little thing that I do.*
2. That Mary would stop being so angry.
3. That we have biweekly date nights and start being more playful with each other again.
4. That we have a more fulfilling sexual relationship.
5. That Mary compliment and affirm me more.

As you can see, their goals were very different. Most of Lou's goals were about Mary changing, and most of Mary's were lofty and somewhat philosophical. Now before you think their marriage is a lost cause, let us assure you that it is not uncommon for couples to present with very different agendas in counseling. After many years as marriage counselors, we have grown to realize that it is not as important what each person wants in the marriage, but rather *why* they want it.

Mary started sharing her why's first. She stated that she did not want to work in their family business because she was tired of feeling responsible for taking care of Lou. It seemed that Mary was having trouble forgiving Lou for the past, and she felt she could not trust him be a responsible provider all on his own. She wanted to spend her time and energy taking care of her children and herself. She expressed guilt feelings for not being there for her children earlier in the marriage when she was working in the business.

As Mary started to share, she began to cry. Her voice softened, and she began to pour out stories of how her life was as a child growing up in a home where she felt responsible for making her parents happy. She had one of many regressive reflections during her counseling. She started feeling the pain of her childhood as if she were back there actually experiencing it. Lou got to see firsthand how painful it was for her. He began to feel her pain with her. She shared stories of her brother's addiction, how she took care of him and often protected her parents from the truth about his problems. It did not take long for Lou to see why it was so important for Mary not to feel overburdened with financial responsibility and the pressure to fix everything.

Lou also relived painful childhood memories and had a few regressive reflections of his own. Mary sat by his side and supported him. She developed a better understanding of the little boy who never felt good enough and who acted out to get attention from his parents.

Even though they were "revisioning" each other, there was still a great deal of resistance to change. Both appeared to be waiting for the other one to act first. No one wanted to be the first to take the risk. This is where the concept of intentionality comes in.

Intentionality

Intentionality is a concept that is used a great deal in self-help groups involving addiction. The definition of *intentionality* is *the ability to think and act in a healing way no matter how you feel.* "Fake it till you make it" is the more colloquial term for this notion. Alcoholics Anonymous teaches us that even if we do not feel like walking past the bar door, even when we are dying for a drink, we are to resist it anyway. After a while, our feelings will follow our behavior.

Many AA participants refer to this as "white-knuckle sobriety." This means staying sober by an act of your will, not by your emotions. We feel that many couples could use "white-knuckle matrimony." In marriage, intentionality is consciously purposing to change a negative behavior whether you have loving feelings for your mate or not. When couples change their behavior, the positive emotions can follow. As you learn to incorporate intentionality in your relationship, you are ready to move to the next stage of marriage, *Transformation*.

Stage 4: The Transformation Stage

When couples reach Transformation, their souls begin to shift. They no longer act on feelings and emotions, but rather, choose to use certain skills and tools to aid in better marital interaction. They learn to deal with their reactivity and negative soul impressions and form new ideas about their spouse. No longer are couples tempted to make up realities about their partner. If they slip back into this old behavior, they know the quick road out. Couples lose that selfish edge they once had, and emotionally or physically leaving is no longer a pondered or real option. They close escape hatches and stop pursuing other forms of distraction from their marriage. When couples reach this stage, they begin to replicate the 1 Corinthians 13 passage about love. They are patient, kind, and do not boast. They want the best for their spouse. Soul healing love becomes a possible, visible goal on the marital horizon.

As they entered the Transformation Stage, Mary and Lou had to work very hard to *agape,* or unconditionally love each other. *Agape* is love given to a person whether or not he or she deserves it. It is given simply because the giver chooses to give it. God gives His children unconditional love. His gift cannot be earned and is not deserved, yet He still chooses to give it.

Mary had a hard time feeling she could give Lou unconditional love. The things he had done in the past haunted her soul and inhibited her ability to trust. This wounded Lou because he felt that Mary would hold his past sins against him forever. When she would try to talk about his drunken binges and spending sprees, he would quote her scriptures about forgiveness. He told her repeatedly that God could not forgive her if she would not forgive him. This form of "spiritual extortion" caused Mary to resent Lou and withhold love and grace from him even more. Acting intentionally with unconditional love was one of the hardest pieces of work this couple did. This kind of love involved stretching beyond their own selfishness. It also involved giving presents that were emotional and behavioral, as well as literal gifts to each other. This kind of caring between couples needs to be supported by the supernatural power of prayer.

We agreed to pray with and for this couple, and ask that the Lord would help them to act lovingly and be open to God's leading, *even if they didn't feel like it.* They both "faked it till they made it," and with the Lord's help, they began to see each other through different eyes. Their behavior not only began to change, but their hearts changed, as well. They had both a first and second order change.

First and Second Order Change

In family therapy, we look for two specific measures of change: One is behavioral, and the other is attitudinal. Behavioral change actually involves changing or reconstructing your behavior to reach a desired goal. This kind of change answers the question, are you acting differently?

Second order change, however, is a *change of attitude.* The operative question here is, do you feel differently? This implies a change of the heart. Your behavior is different because you want it to be, because your heart dictates that it change. This behavior change is an outgrowth of a change in your emotions and beliefs. We call this a soul shift, or soul change.

Mary tried very hard to make a first order change. She was "faking it" and "making it" as hard as she could. She shared childhood pain, acted in a loving manner to Lou, checked her reactivity and old brainers, and tried to be as intentional as possible. Mary had a problem, however; faking her feelings was very hard for her. She had trouble feeling like a phony. Authenticity and truth were two very important concepts in her life. I had to assure her many times that the goal of this process was not dishonesty or loss of integrity due to phoniness. The goal was simply to act lovingly and Christlike, and pray for the feelings to follow. Mary reluctantly agreed to try these new behaviors on faith.

With God's help, Mary was able to spot most of her reactivity and eventually stop it. She was able to trust the Lord and give Lou *agape*. By acting in obedience and love, her heart did indeed begin to change. One of the first feelings that came back was her genuine gratitude and appreciation for Lou. Compliments and encouragement began to naturally flow from her. This started to heal Lou's wound of never feeling good enough, so his soul began to shift, as well. Both of them began to act and feel more loving toward each other.

It took a while for Mary to fight through her resistance to acting phony, but it paid off in the healing of both her and Lou's souls. Their relationship then moved to the final stage of marriage, the best one, the one we call Soul Healing Love.

Stage 5: Soul Healing Love Stage

This is the stage that makes all the struggles worthwhile. This is when couples have knowledge, acceptance, appreciation, and gratitude for each other. Instead of seeing their mate as a demon of destruction, they get in touch with what bonded them in the first place. By giving each other God's unconditional love, couples create a safe environment for mutual sharing. Both feel freer to share their soul pain. This sharing helps them develop a deeper understanding of themselves and their spouse. Couples start "revisioning" each other as soul healers, not soul wounders. They develop compassion and empathy for the wounds in each other's souls and commit to healing them. No longer do they see the face of their perpetrators on their partner; instead, they see an innocent, wounded child, and they want to nurture and heal that child.

Seeing the Wounded Child's Face

During the stage of soul healing love, couples start by seeing each other as wounded children instead of difficult, frustrating adults. This "revisioning" each other is extremely helpful for couples in trouble, like Mary and Lou. Remember when they first came in to see us? They were full of anger and fear. Like most desperate couples, both "made up" that the other had evil or less than honorable intentions. They tended to reduce the problems in their marriage to selfishness on their mate's part. Blaming each other became a way of life for them. This only reinforced their negative image of each other, as well as blinding them from the part they themselves played in the marital conflict.

As Mary and Lou's paradigm shifted, they started to see the wounded child's face on each other, they stopped seeing their mate's motives so negatively, and they began to understand why each acted the way they did. They could also own their own responsibility for how they affected their relationship. *Koinonia*, or mutual empathy, began to emerge between them. They began to feel each other's pain as if it were their own. A shared respect grew between these two that was rooted in a deep understanding for what each had gone through in life.

Lou listened with compassion and empathy while Mary poured out childhood wounds of a little blonde girl who had to grow up too fast. It was much more difficult for him to withdraw, get angry, or become passive-aggressive at an innocent, wounded little girl who just wanted everyone to be happy. Likewise, it was hard for Mary to put an uncaring, unloving face on a little boy who got in trouble while simply looking for attention and love from his family.

So, the hurting little girl who tried to over-caretake everyone, and the wounded little boy who never felt good enough, finally started seeing each other as friends. Caring for each other's soul was no longer a chore or an act of the will. It became their utmost desire. Both wanted to listen as their partner shared. Both felt it was important to minister soul healing love to each other. They became friends.

It is important to note here that *philia*, or friendship, was a logical progression for a couple after *eros*, erotic love, and *agape*, unconditional love. We interviewed many Christian couples who had been married over forty years and asked them to tell us what they thought was the most important ingredient in marriage. To our surprise, they did not say it was any great sacrificial giving or moving revelation. It was simply being friends. Many of them spoke of caring, concern, and support, but the answers boiled down to pure and simple friendship, *philia*. We see so many couples who marry, bear children, buy homes, and share the daily grind with each other, but who are not friends. It is no wonder why so many marriages are suffering today.

Mary and Lou's friendship began to blossom when they started seeing each other through different eyes. Learning about the stages of marriage helped them understand how their relationship had become stagnant. After their many insights, they were ready to learn to communicate the really negative emotions they were feeling. They were also ready to see what they did to hurt each other, learn to share this information in a healthy way, and then ask for and grant forgiveness. The next chapter shows you how to do this, step by step.

CHAPTER 8

WHAT'S EATING YOU AND WHY

We have already learned that the state of being in love is more of a myth than a reality. It is based on projection not truth. Remember, projection is defined as the act of visualizing an idea in our minds as an objective reality.[1] We also learned previously that we tend to make up realities about our partners. In relationships we see things through our own clouded perspective, which may not be completely accurate. Projection can also be a way in which we cloud our perspective and attribute to another person or object feelings, thoughts, or attitudes that are present in ourselves. In the Romantic Stage of a relationship, we have a tendency to project positive characteristics onto our partner. In the Power Struggle Stage, we tend to project the negative characteristics. By doing this, we do not have to own or deal with these characteristics within ourselves. When a problem arises in marriage, our tendency is to look outside of our own psyches, and project blame onto our spouses. This may blind us from seeing what is really eating us in our marriage and why.

Fred and Ethel's Story of Projection

Fred was a thirty-year-old bachelor. He came into our counseling office because his girlfriend of two years had just broken up with him. He was not eating or sleeping, and was so depressed that he had trouble getting out of bed in the mornings.

"I feel completely lost and empty without Ethel. What am I going to do? She was my whole life. She inspired me. Now I can't even go to work."

Upon further questioning, we found that Fred saw Ethel as the life force or life energy in their relationship. Fred was raised in a very stoic, conservative, sexually shaming home, so he was very shy and inhibited. Ethel was very sensual and expressive. He was stiff and unaffectionate. She was warm and openly affectionate. He was too serious. She could laugh and play. No wonder he felt more complete and whole with her; she possessed everything he had repressed. When she walked out of his life, all of his *eros*, or life energy, went with her. Fred felt dead inside. In order to help him heal, he had to learn that he, too, possessed the characteristics that Ethel brought into the relationship. They were just lost in his unconscious mind, or repressed. It was easier and safer for Fred to project these characteristics on Ethel than to develop them within himself.

As we saw earlier in this text, couples often do this early in their relationship. Later, however, they tend to project the negative characteristics from their psyche onto their partner. As Fred started to look inside himself, find these lost parts, and act on them, he began to feel more whole. This helped him get over the loss of Ethel and learn to love again.

Projection and Relationships

Because relationship theorists say that 80 percent of all communication is projection, it would behoove us to examine our communication in order to separate fantasy from reality, or truth from projection. These same relationship theorists say that what we despise most in others is really a projection. We hate the most in others the negative qualities that we possess within ourselves.

Is there a characteristic that you really scorn in others? Say that you despise arrogant people. Could it be that you have a small piece of this arrogance within yourself? Seeing your own despised psyche personified in another creates discomfort and anxiety. You feel uneasy or troubled. These are unpleasant emotions, so you have disdain for the bearer of the traits that bring out such angst in you. It is much easier for you to greatly despise in others that which you may see in small portion within yourself, because if you see it within yourself, you may have to own it, and then you would have to do something about it. Rather than working toward healing within yourself, it is easier to put this off on someone else. Who better to project onto than your own spouse? After all, he or she already contains some of the positive projections of your repressed psyches, just as Ethel did with Fred. That is why couples fall in love with each other in the first place. It becomes almost second nature to "give," or project, these unpleasant or negative characteristics onto your partner, as well.

Communication and Projections

Because you now know that projection is a large part of communication in a relationship, then it is safe to assume that the main things you dislike about your partner are also present within yourself. You also repress those traits that are not sanctioned in your home. Remember that Fred repressed his outgoing nature when he was younger, because his family did not approve of, or encourage him to develop his social side. They praised his serious, academic, quiet qualities. One could even say it wasn't safe for him to be social or outgoing when he grew up.

In the beginning of the relationship with Ethel, he felt safe and complete, as he was allowed to explore these repressed parts of himself in the presence of one so gifted in the social arena. As the relationship progressed, however, her display of social prowess only served to show him his lack in this area. It also made him feel unconsciously uncomfortable and even anxious, as she so openly displayed that which was not valued or supported in his home. This caused him to project his own lack of social graces onto her. He started accusing her of having poor social skills. This is ironic because her outgoing nature was what had initially attracted him to her in the first place.

"Why do you talk so much at parties?" he would ask accusingly. "People think it's rude when they can't get a word in edgewise. No one likes a blabbermouth."

"Blabbermouth!" Ethel would retort. "Look at you! If I didn't talk, the group would die of boredom. You just sit there and never interact in the conversation."

The very things that had attracted Fred and Ethel to each other, the very things that had complimented their sense of wholeness, had become the very things they had conflict about. The things that had completed them now repelled them.

As our theory of projection unfolds, we see that Fred had a repressed socialite within him, and Ethel had a hidden shy girl inside her. Seeing their partner act differently from themselves caused them to have anxiety. Rather than express this as an internal struggle, most couples share this as criticism, just as Fred and Ethel did.

To handle this type of conflict more constructively, each person needs to own their own part in their projections. This is called *"leaning into your projection."* If Fred could cultivate his own social nature, and Ethel could own and accept her inhibited side, then these two would bring more compassion and understanding to the table of relational discord. They would each be less apt to criticize the other, and more predisposed to share genuine feelings in conflict. They would also learn the cardinal rule of relationships: *You are not your partner, and your partner is not you.*

Take a moment and think about what you dislike most in your mate. Do you possess this characteristic in some measure in yourself? Can you own this? Does this give you more understanding about why your mate does what he or she does? As partners begin to apply this principle, they can learn to heal the strife and discord in their marriages.

Learning to Repress

How did we lose this natural part of ourselves in the first place? As humans, we were born with certain innate characteristics. As babies, we were loving, lovable, and playful. We were naturally expressive. When we needed something, we screamed for it. We had no reservations about crying at two A.M. when we were hungry. As adults, however, we have learned that certain traits were promoted, while others were discouraged. These characteristics were not necessarily what might be best for our particular *bend*, or nature. Take Fred, for example. His parents could have really helped him by encouraging his social skills and developing his extroverted side more. But instead, they touted his more serious strengths, because they, too, were serious.

Proverbs 22:6 says, "Train a child in the *way* he should go, and when he is old he will not turn from it" (NIV, emphasis ours). The Hebrew word for *way* is *derek*, meaning nature, course of life, mode of action, custom, manner, or bend. What this verse is saying is that we should train up children according to *their* mode or *their* bend. We are to train them based on *their* predisposed manner. We are to train them according to the characteristics that best support who *they* are. Many Christian parents misinterpret this passage to read, "Train a child in the way that I, as his or her parent, think the child should go." This is not accurate scripturally, nor is it good or healthy for them emotionally and psychologically.

What if your entire family were accountants, and you were expected to follow in their footsteps, yet you were greatly talented at art, and hated math? What if you came from a family of athletes, but you were a weak, slightly built child? What if you were an overachieving perfectionist and your parents insisted on pushing you too much to succeed? They could actually foster obsessive-compulsive neurosis within you.

This is what has happened to many individuals today. Their *way* was not found, and their *bend* was not supported. Because of this, they became only shadows of their true selves. They were split off from many of their worthy attributes. This splitting off is the seedbed of much of their relational conflict as adults.

Parents are responsible for finding their child's *way* and helping the child follow it. Rather than force a child's round psyche into life's square hole, parents need to ask God, the Creator of these children, to guide them. If parents try too hard to put their own, or society's, unhealthy agenda on their children, they can cause their children to repress their most godly qualities. Here are some examples of attitudes and statements that you may have heard as a child that would cause you to repress or hide your true self.

- *Children should be seen and not heard.* This statement causes us to repress our ability to verbally articulate our thoughts, feelings, and actions.
- *Children should be quiet and not make noise.* This statement causes us to split -off from our ability to articulate and verbalize.
- *Children should not act silly.* This statement causes us to repress our natural, childish, joyful, and playful side. We become very serious.
- *If you can't say anything nice, don't say anything at all.* This statement causes us to split from the truth within us.
- *Don't be sexual. Don't be sensual. Sex is dirty.* This statement cause us to repress the normal, sensual side of our humanness.
  Some messages are indigenous to gender.
- *Nice girls don't flirt.* This statement causes women to repress their natural mating energy and femininity.
- *Loudness, yelling, or anger isn't ladylike.* This statement causes women to repress their assertiveness.

- ◆ *Girls don't play sports. Boys are the athletes.* This statement causes women to split off from their athletic ability.
- ◆ *Nice girls don't get angry.* This statement causes women to split off from the expression of their hurt and pain.
- ◆ *Big boys don't cry.* This statement causes men to repress their sensitivity and compassion.
- ◆ *Boys are supposed to be tough.* This statement causes men to repress their pain.
- ◆ *Boys should not have needs.* This statement causes men to ignore their own soul needs and never show vulnerability.
- ◆ *Nice guys finish last.* This statement causes men to repress their kind side and show more of their competitiveness.

Families were not the only source of repression. Culture and society have also played a big part in dictating some of these damaging gender rules. My (Bev's) grandmother died at 104 years old. She grew up in the hills of Tennessee, believing that a woman's place was "barefoot, pregnant, and chained to the stove." My mother grew up in the 1930s, when men were believed to have the brains, and women were the domestic ones, or caretakers. The idea of women going to college was unheard of in her small Southern hometown. A college education was for men, not women. Why would a woman get an education if she was going to marry? This caused the women in my family to repress their abilities, drive, and ambition, and sometimes even ignore the call of God on their lives.

Our generation is coming to terms with the war between the genders. Our children have a better chance of not repressing parts of their natural *bend*, because of society's less slanted structure. Not only do we have men taking time off from work to drive the kids to the pediatrician, we also have women who are the pediatricians! The change in cultural stereotypes can bring a great deal of healing to our lost selves.

Finding Our Lost Selves

We need to acknowledge what parts of us are wounded and lost, and how this happened. We can work on healing those wounds by allowing the repressed aspects of our souls to surface. Then we can bring them under the control of the Holy Spirit, and allow God's mighty power to help channel these feelings, emotions, and attributes in a healthy direction.

If we stay fearful of these lost parts, the dark, forbidden shadow of our souls will rear its ugly head in our marriage. In courtship, the appearance of our disallowed self that was contained within our partner made us feel complete, but eventually that which is forbidden starts to scare us. When this happens, we attack our partner, and project all the forbidden parts of our souls onto him or her. By doing this, we never have to face our own repressed aspects and learn to heal them. Projecting is about making our problem belong to our spouse. We project our psychic mess onto our spouse so that we do not have to take responsibility for facing our own discomfort and fear.

An example of this type of projection was played out early in our own marriage. Tom was working as a pastor, and I was working part-time, in private practice, as a therapist. Our first child, Mandy, was fifteen months old. It was the end of a busy day. I had picked her up from the babysitter and was preparing supper. It began to get late, and Tom was still not home. Six o'clock rolled around. I called the church, but the phones had already been switched to the answering machine. It was now 6:30, and no Tom. Dinner was getting soggy, and Mandy started to whine. In an effort to pacify her, I gave her some Cheerios, which she promptly began to throw on the floor. The dog came in and ate all the Cheerios on the floor and her highchair tray. She began to scream, the oven buzzer went off, and the phone rang. It was a phone solicitor wanting me to be charitable. Needless to say, I was not feeling charitable at that time. I lost it! I fussed at the caller, then fussed at the dog, and then fussed at my precious hungry child. As you can imagine, I was feeling like a failure as a mother, a cook, and a Christian. The internal angst of my guilt was eating me alive. About 7:10, my husband arrived to our chaotic home. I launched into him with a vengeance.

"Where have you been?" I whined. "Why didn't you call to say you were going to be late?" Before he could even catch his breath, I was busy projecting all my guilty feelings onto him.

"What kind of husband would leave his family stranded at suppertime? What kind of daddy would leave his poor baby hungry without so much as a phone call?"

In two minutes, I had successfully "given" Tom all of my guilt and agony about being a bad person. I no longer had to deal with these awful feelings, because my displaced anger at Tom allowed me to project all of them onto him. You can just imagine how he felt being welcomed into his home with this! It goes without saying that we did not have a good time in the Rodgers household that evening.

We have traveled the hard road that couples take as they learn to "lean into their projections," rather than spewing them onto each other. It has taken many years on our part to really look inside ourselves and see the ugliness that we would rather "give away" to each other. We began to really look at what was eating us in our relationship and why. For many couples, this can be a difficult task.

Fear and Repression

Most people have a hard time owning their lost or repressed parts. They also refuse to own any of their sin nature because the guilt is much too hard to bear. The answer to all of life's struggles for them is to be better, work harder, or serve more. There is no room for God's grace to abound, because they are using their perfectionism and determination instead. Guilt and shame will not allow them to own the dark parts of their soul, so they have to have somewhere to put them. Ah yes, how about their mate, the perfect hiding place? They give their mate all of their ugliness in the form of a projection.

Projection works just like a movie projector that puts forth an image on the screen. We put our forbidden self on the movie screen of our mate's psyche, and thus we see our lost parts portrayed or enacted by someone else. This gets us off the hook from owning and healing our own dark shadow. It also allows us to continue hiding or repressing that prohibited part of ourselves. It is then safe to say that we project onto our partner that which we fear seeing in ourselves.

Projections Take the Form of Anger

The main way we project our own mess onto our partner is through anger. Anger is usually our mate's retaliatory response, as well. We will either become furious with our spouse for possessing the same behaviors that we despise in ourselves, or furious with ourselves for our own dark spots. Either way, the paramount emotion shown is anger.

Anger, however, is not really the main culprit. It is only a secondary emotion, usually felt in response to a more primary feeling, which means that anger is more of the response than the root of a particular situation. Submerged under anger are four basic feelings that help define or give purpose to our rage. Chances are, if you are feeling anger, you can trace it to any of these four emotions. They are as follows:

> Guilt
> Inferiority (or Inadequacy)
> Fear
> Trauma (or Pain)

We have developed an acronym for these underlying emotions so that you can easily trace them to their root cause. We chose the word **GIFT** because we feel that it is a **GIFT** to you, and to your spouse, to identify the root of your wrath. If you respond to your mate in anger, it tends to create a defensive or angry response from them in return. Healthy communication is thwarted, and conflict goes unresolved. By tracing the root of your anger, you may be able to share it more effectively with your mate. By using the **GIFT** acronym, you will have a format to follow in tracing the root of your rage.

Proverbs 14:29 says, "A wise man controls his temper. He knows that anger causes mistakes" (TLB). Proverbs 15:1 says, "A gentle answer turns away wrath, but harsh words cause quarrels" (TLB). The purpose of the **GIFT** acronym is to help you communicate your frustration, irritation, and rage more honestly. We have seen that if one partner relates in anger, then the other is much less likely to really hear what he or she is saying. If, however, that same mate responds by sharing what is really bothering them (that is, guilt, inferiority, fear, or pain) then their partner is much more apt to listen and change.

At first, you may resist believing that anger is really veiling these four basic feelings. But if you look further, you may be able to see the root cause of your rage. When someone cuts you off in traffic, how do you feel? It moves you to even the score, perhaps to pull in front of them, maybe block their way, name call, or even gesture at them. You feel disregarded, less than, cutoff, put down. Does this sound like inferiority to you? Another example may be when a relative calls and whines that you have not called them in a while. Many times you respond with defensiveness and anger, when what you really feel is guilt. Think about what makes you mad in your marriage relationship. Now look for the root. Isn't it found in your **GIFT**?

Levels of Anger

There are five basic levels of anger. Almost every time a couple tells us what they do not like about their marriage, one of these is mentioned. They are as follows:

1. **Annoyance.** This is the bothersome feeling you get about your partner's tedious trifling behavior. They are not monumental behaviors, but rather persistent nuisances

that are troublesome. An example may be when your spouse squeezes the toothpaste from the bottom and not the top of the tube, as you would prefer.

2. **Irritation.** This is the impatient sense you get about your partner's more aggravating habits that excite or bug you. An example is when your spouse always leaves crumbs on the counter after he or she makes a sandwich.

3. **Frustration.** This is the feeling of dissatisfaction, often accompanied by anxiety or depression. It is usually based on a sense that needs are unfulfilled or problems are unresolved. An example is when your spouse is late for an appointment and does not call.

4. **Anger.** This is the strong feeling of displeasure or belligerence aroused by real or supposed wrong. These feelings are usually sudden and can be accompanied by an impulse to retaliate. An example may be when your spouse does not help with the chores or yard work after repeated requests, and you explode at him or her.

5. **Rage.** This is the violent fury that burns within us when we feel a soul injustice has occurred. It can also be described as explosive anger, or anger out of control, often rooted in reactivity. The urge to retaliate is very strong. Rage can, however, be more passive-aggressive than explosive. Name calling or verbal abuse can be an outgrowth of rage. Having an affair can be a passive-aggressive way to act out rage.

As you can see, different levels of anger warrant different levels of emotion. It is helpful to identify the level you are feeling, so that you can more accurately assess your needs in conflict. Rageful, abusive name calling for leaving crumbs on the counter is over-reactive for such an offense. By identifying your level of anger, you can give a situation only the amount of anger it deserves. You also learn that all marriages have little annoyances and irritations, and to waste valuable energy on these trifling behaviors expends energy that is needed for the more important things in a marriage.

I (Bev) once had a client who yelled and screamed at her husband, in a fit of rage, for putting the dinner forks in the salad fork section of the silverware drawer. My advice to her was "Get over it! Suck it up!" All couples have little things that irritate each other. You cannot take two completely different people and put them in a house together without some kind of annoyance or irritation. People are just too different. To spend all of your emotional energy on these things drains you of energy needed for the more important issues in marriage. We want couples to save their energy for the things that really matter in a relationship. Typically these are the deeper emotions in our psyche. The following is an exercise we designed to help couples get in touch with these deeper emotions.

The GIFT Exercise

Rob and Laura came into therapy because their unhealthy anger was destroying their relationship. Rob was a salesman who traveled all week and returned home on the weekends. When he entered the house, he would rage at Laura and the children because the house was a mess and there were toys in the driveway and the garage so that he could not park his car inside. At one point he even ran over the toys in the driveway to "teach his kids a lesson."

Laura said that she tried to keep the house clean but she had many other responsibilities, as well. She had to take care of all of the household chores and run a small jewelry business. Rob just did not understand how busy her days were. In a typical day she might drive the girls to ballet lessons, take phone calls from her ailing mother, as well as bathe the dog and go back to school to get something that one of the kids had forgotten. There was always something else to do. Laura was tired of being criticized and accused of being a poor time manager and a lazy housekeeper and said that if Rob did not learn to control his anger, she wanted a divorce. She had even seen an attorney before she scheduled an appointment with us.

Now, why, you may ask, can't she just clean the house? Isn't that a simple request? Another one of our sayings in the Soul Healing Love Model is: *Requirement equals resistance.*

Requirement Equals Resistance

In the Soul Healing Love Model, one of the main principles is "requirement equals resistance." If you require something, if you make it mandatory, people will resist doing it more than if you gave them the freedom of choice. This frustrating aspect of human behavior is troublesome for marriage, but it is as old as the story of Adam and Eve in the Garden of Eden. In the Genesis account of Paradise, Adam and Eve could have anything to eat that they wanted. There was only one food that was prohibited, the fruit of the tree of the knowledge of good and evil. This prohibition made them want it all the more.

If you have a hard time accepting this generalization, think about this. Let's say that your neighbor picks up your paper and places it on your porch every afternoon by five o'clock. You are very grateful for his thoughtfulness. But then, one day you walk over and tell him that you are coming home early and you want him to bring your paper in at three o'clock instead of five. Do you honestly think that your neighbor will oblige you? We think not. The requirement you placed on him will cause him to resist your request. When you take away your neighbor's free will, he will be more likely to withstand your appeal. This has been human nature since the Garden of Eden.

This principle played out in Rob and Laura's relationship. Rob wanted (required) Laura to spend more time attending to things around the house. She resisted by telling him the litany of things she had to do and asking him to help her. He then resisted helping her, saying that she needed to manage her time better. These conflicts usually ended in screaming matches, and since Rob was bigger and louder, he typically dominated Laura and she would seethe with resentment because there was no resolution in sight.

When they came in for their session, Laura started to talk about how defeated she was and how Rob's anger had crushed her. He immediately leaned forward and started to yell at her. When I (Bev) intervened, he started to yell at me. "Rob, you need to calm down. This type of reactivity is not working in your relationship," I said.

"Why should I?" was his surly retort.

Before I could think about it, these words rolled off my tongue: "Because nobody in this room is more lonely than you right now!"

"Wow. You're right," was Rob's softer response as he calmed down and listened to what I had to say.

"Rob, this is not working for you. You want to get your needs met and have a wife and kids who are close to you and care about you, yet you are doing the very things that will push them away. From now on, when you get angry, I want you to grab your thumb."

Now, the thumb is not a mystical object of focus, it is just a way to get an angry person to think about something cerebral so that they can redirect their rage. It is like counting to ten or walking around the block. I told Rob, "Grab your thumb the moment you feel yourself getting angry. When you do this, you will see four fingers in front of you. They represent:

Guilt,
Inferiority,
Fear, and
Trauma (hurt).

"Instead of raging, you will determine which primary emotion is triggered and talk calmly about it to Laura."

We instructed Rob to share this emotion by simply saying, "When you… I feel…" This method of confrontation has been around for a long time and has been proven to soften arguments and help couples resolve conflict. To my surprise, Rob agreed to do this.

In the next session, Laura reported that Rob came home a little early from a trip and the house was not quite as clean as she wanted it to be. Rob grabbed his thumb and *calmly* walked toward her and said, "When you do not have the house clean when I return home from a busy week, I feel... *inferior.*" He then looked at his protruding fingers, as if to figure out the root of his rage. "I feel like I am not important and that my needs do not matter to you." Rob was so calm and composed that Laura was shocked. She stood there for a moment not believing her eyes or her ears. Finally, she could actually hear Rob because his rage no longer drowned out his need. She even jokingly said, "Who are you and where are the aliens that have my husband—and are they planning to bring him back?" We all got a laugh out of this. But then things turned more serious. Laura actually heard Rob as a result of the GIFT Exercise.

"Rob," she said, "I never meant to make you feel unimportant. I had no idea you thought your needs did not matter. They do, but I'm just so busy that sometimes things get in the way. I will try to make you feel that you matter to us." This was very healing for Rob because he finally felt heard. It was healing for Laura because he no longer hovered over her in a rage. Rob said that the GIFT Exercise helped him do several things that changed the way he dealt with anger:

1. It slowed things down so that his anger could not fester into rage.
2. It caused him to re-context his anger and determine the root of it. This helped him better understand his feelings.
3. The root helped him see why this made him so angry. Men do not like to feel inferior or unimportant. It makes them feel too vulnerable. They typically translate this vulnerability into anger. Identifying this helped Rob stop raging and start talking from his heart about what was really going on inside of him.

This simple tool helped this couple stop screaming and start talking. Instead of getting angry and hurling insults, they were better equipped to share their true feelings and thus get their needs met. The GIFT Exercise created a paradigm shift for this couple that changed the landscape of their marriage. We could have left them with just this, but they had the urge to go deeper.

Laura and Rob lived in a neighborhood with six other couples. All of the husbands traveled through the week for work, so the women were used to their husbands coming home only on weekends. Laura was curious because, out of all of the couples, Rob was the only husband who got upset when the house was not clean. Some of the guys actually helped their kids clean up. Laura wondered why the mess was such a toxic trigger for Rob. In order to help this couple find out the answer, we developed an exercise that enables couples to dig deeper into their psyches and see why they are so reactive.

The Digging Deeper Exercise

The Digging Deeper Exercise allows you to do several things:

- Dig deeper into your psyche and identify triggers in your current relationship.
- Understand the feelings these triggers evoke, or more basically, determine why you are so reactive.
- Attach those feelings to early childhood wounds.
- Separate family-of-origin issues from patterns in your marriage.
- Determine what you really need in your marriage.

In order to do the Digging Deeper Exercise, you will need to answer five simple questions. They are simple, but not easy, because you will have to dig deep to find the answers. Because this exercise is a spin-off of the GIFT Exercise, simply repeat the GIFT by answering the first two questions.

1. *What is the behavior that my mate does that triggers my anger?*
   When my mate does this, I feel this.
2. *What is the root of my feeling Guilt, Inferiority, Fear, or Trauma (hurt)?*

The third question is where it gets a little harder.

3. *When have I ever felt this feeling before?*

What you are looking for is whether a soul wound has been triggered, and because of what we have learned previously, you will want to ask the question, when *in childhood* have I felt this before?

We asked Rob when he had felt this feeling of inferiority before. "Oh, that's easy to answer," Rob said. "I felt it before last week, and the week before that, and the week before that, well pretty much the whole eighteen years that I have been on the road."

"Rob, can you dig a little deeper?" I asked. This is where the exercise gets its name. "Rob, dig a little deeper in your psyche and tell me when *in childhood* you have felt this before."

This was much more difficult for Rob. He thought for a moment, looked up, and said fearfully, "Oh, no, you're not gonna make me go there, are you?" It was obvious that the question unlocked a painful childhood memory for him.

"No, Rob, I won't make you, but the Lord will help you," I said softly. "The Lord wants you to remember, so that He can help you heal. He will be right here with you as you unpack the wounds of your childhood, and He will give you what you need to heal them." Remember, in Jeremiah 30:17, the Lord says, "I will restore you to health and heal your wounds" (NIV).

For the next few minutes, Rob shared about a very painful situation that had happened when he was a boy. He had a brother who was twelve years older and a sister who was ten years older, and they told him that his parents drank heavily when they grew up. But he remembered his parents as being the pillars of the church. They lived just around the corner and were there every time the doors were open. His dad even kept the grounds and his mom cleaned the pews every Saturday, except for one fateful year.

When Rob was nine years old, his dad got laid off at the mill and struggled to find a job. Rob's mom was so upset by this that she started drinking again. He told us through tears that he remembered walking home from school and dreading going home because he feared that his mother would have passed out on the couch. He would sober her up, clean the filthy house, and make everything look fine so that when his father returned home, he would not know that Mom had been drinking and would not be discouraged in his difficult job search.

"How did you feel then?" I asked Rob.

"Terrible," he said. "I was furious with my mom for letting me and Dad down."

"Did you tell your mom how you felt?" I asked.

"Are you kidding? She was my mom. We didn't talk to her like that. It was disrespectful."

"What did you do when you got angry at your mom?" I questioned.

"Nothing. I just shoved it down and kept on going."

"So you never told your mom how you felt?" I said. "Is that how you handle conflict today?" (This is actually the fourth question in the Digging Deeper Exercise:

4. What is my response?)

"No," Rob said, "I can't stand to hold in my emotions. I swore when I grew up that I would never have to shove things down again."

All of a sudden, Rob got it. He looked like a light bulb had gone off in his head. And he said, "I see it now, all of the anger that I have for my mother, I project onto Laura. I tell her all the things that I wish I could have told my mom, and I give her all the anger that belongs in the past. No wonder I get so mad." As he made this realization, a great deal of emotion came over him.

Laura got emotional, too, as she watched Rob finally connect the dots as to why he was so angry. She said, "Sometimes I actually felt like Rob put someone else's face on me when he would say unfounded things like, 'You don't do anything but sit around all day,' and 'Why are you so lazy?'" Laura knew that she was anything but lazy, and she felt truly that Rob knew this, too, so she could not see why he was so harsh, until that moment. She finally understood that Rob actually put his mother's face on her. All the anger he could not give his mother, he unwittingly unleashed on Laura.

This realization was so overwhelming for Rob that all he could do was cry. Finally, he looked at Laura and whispered, "I'm so sorry. I'm so, so sorry." They both held each other and cried as they realized how reactivity from past soul wounds was destroying their marriage. As their therapist, I cried, too. It was a sacred moment for this couple, and I truly felt like we were on holy ground as they were sharing. We could have stopped there, but we had one more question to complete the exercise.

The last question in the Digging Deeper Exercise is:

5. What do I really need?

Until this point, Rob would say that all he needed was to have the house clean when he came home. This, of course, would be met with resistance, and he and Laura would continue the power struggle. The Digging Deeper Exercise gave this couple a paradigm shift. Rob saw things differently. Instead of simply asking for a clean house, he made a deeper request.

"Laura, I need to know that my needs and requests are important to you. I need to know that I matter," Rob said softly.

"Oh, Robby, I had no idea that was what you needed," Laura said as she touched his cheek gently. "And to think that all of this time, I thought that you were just trying to be a controlling jerk." Again, we all got a little chuckle from her candor. "This makes so much sense to me, Robby. Now I know why you get so upset. I get it. Not that it is okay for you to yell, but I get it."

Apparently, Laura saw things differently, as well. The Digging Deeper Exercise changed the whole environment of Rob and Laura's relationship. We gave them some guidelines in this sharing. They could not interrupt, only listen until it was their turn to speak. They also had to listen with empathy. They had to practice *koinonia*, or hearing each other's pain as if it were their own. As they continued to do this exercise, they began to hear the deeper meaning behind each other's anger. This brought a new understanding to them. Sharing, without so much rage, helped both of them really listen to each other. They both could hear each other's needs for the first time in their relationship. They could then work toward ways of meeting those needs, in order to heal each other's soul wounds, as well as heal themselves.

I saw them a few months later for a checkup, and they were doing quite well. I asked Laura how Rob was doing with his anger. She said that he was greatly improving. Then she told me about one weekend when he came home early and she heard him yelling in the driveway. She said that she panicked and had an old brainer right on the spot. She ran to the gate of the yard because she was sure that the new Rob had disappeared and the old angry Rob was back. (This is a common fear for couples who engage in a radical change.) To her surprise, when she got to the gate, she saw Rob actually helping the kids pick up their toys. He had yelled not in anger, but because he was playing ball with them as he cleaned. Laura was so overwhelmed that she started to cry. Rob ran to the gate and said, "Laura, what's wrong?" "Nothing," Laura said. "Absolutely nothing. Everything is just right."

I asked Laura what went through her mind as she stood there watching her husband help her children like all of the other husbands on the street.

"You really want to know?" she asked.

"Sure," I replied.

"At that moment I thought that I could have missed this. If I had not done the hard work of soul healing, I… we… would have missed this. This is what I have always prayed for, and it is finally here," Laura shared with much gratitude in her voice.

Let's walk through the five questions in the Digging Deeper Exercise so that you can learn to do it in your own marriage:

1. *What is the behavior that my mate does that triggers my anger?*

When you do this, I feel this.

2. *Identify the root of this anger using the GIFT Exercise.*

    Guilt
    Inferiority
    Fear
    Trauma (hurt)

3. *Ask yourself, when have I ever felt this feeling before?*

When in childhood have you felt this feeling before? Many of us do not have a lot of memories from childhood. Some may have even repressed some painful ones. If this is the case with you, pray and ask the Lord to help you access memories that will help you heal. We have found that the Holy Spirit is a gentleman and He will not give you more than you can handle. Ask and He will show you what you need to know.

4. *What do I do when feel I this feeling?*

Do you yell and criticize? Do you withdraw and pout? Do you try to lecture and control? If you, like Rob, had to repress feelings from childhood, then you may spew them out onto your spouse with a vengeance. You will want to get in touch with these emotions so that they do not cause harm in your marriage.

5. What do I really need?

You will want to dig deeper when you are determining your need. Often what looks like something simple, like cleaning the house, may actually be something much more profound. Look for the deeper need because it is tied to the healing of your soul. As you state your needs in marriage, you will want to turn them into behavior change requests and set goals to meet them. We will show you how to do this in Chapter Ten, but first we want to help you deal with some of the really hard stuff of marriage.

This next chapter teaches you ways to discuss painful, soul-murdering wounds that couples inflict upon each other and how to move to a healing place of forgiveness.

CHAPTER 9

COMMUNICATING THE HARD STUFF

*I*n the past few decades, marriage researchers have studied the interaction of married couples in order to determine what communication styles lead to divorce and which ones promote a healthy, lasting marriage. Dr. John Gottman, professor of psychology at the University of Washington, Seattle, is perhaps one of America's foremost marriage researchers. In one of his most noted studies, he looked at the interactions of two hundred marital couples via videotape for a period of ten years. As he examined verbal and nonverbal communication patterns, he was able to tabulate these patterns and determine which ones led couples to divorce and which ones were present in couples who stayed married. By doing this, he was able to "crack the code" for marital communication and interaction. Because of his work, he can watch a two-minute video of a couple and predict with over 90 percent accuracy whether the couple will stay married or get a divorce.

It is important to note that Gottman and his team found that all couples fight and that the absence of conflict is not a predictor of marital longevity. So, thinking that you are doing well if you do not fight may be very unhealthy for your marriage. Gottman found that it was the *way* the couple fought or resolved conflict that determined whether or not their marriage would last.

The most common "hot buttons" about which couples experience conflict are *money, sex, in-laws, roles, child-rearing, jealousy over time spent outside the marriage, and religion.* We call these Toxic Subjects because they typically create a fight-or-flight response in people, which means they will either withdraw and shut down, or fight about these issues. Irreconcilable differences around these topics are commonly listed as the main reasons for divorce in our society.

We want to share some of Gottman's findings with you in hopes that you may prevent dysfunctional patterns from infiltrating your marital communication. These negative behaviors can actually exacerbate marital struggles and foster even more opposition between spouses. If you find that you and your spouse have already fallen into some poor communication traps, we will show you a way out. Gottman's predictors of divorce are discussed below.[1]

Predictors of Divorce
Stonewalling/Withdrawal

Stonewalling is withdrawing, or shutting down, and refusing to deal with conflict. It can be done both emotionally, by closing off and refusing to talk, or physically, by walking away or leaving. Gottman found that stonewalling is typically done more by husbands than wives. He also found that it is normative for the wife to take the emotional responsibility for the marriage. This means that she is the one who typically brings up the thorny issues that need to be negotiated and resolved, and she is the one who persists until the discussion ends in a satisfactory resolution, or a screaming match.

Many times this can be irritating to husbands who, Gottman found, were much less willing to bring conflict to the table. Men were more likely to ignore or live with what they consider minor disappointments than risk a big argument. Typically, the only issue men will bring to the table is the question, "Why can't I get more sex?" which can also be frustrating for women.

When wives do bring up conflicting issues, husbands have a tendency to avoid or minimize them and treat them like they are "no big deal." This brings out the pursuer in the wife who becomes angry because she feels that her concerns are being dismissed. As a result, she may maximize her issues and become critical, reciting a litany of what is wrong in the marriage in order to convince her husband that a serious problem exists. Thus we see the number-two predictor of divorce, which is *criticism*.

Criticism

Because men are more likely to avoid conflict, we see women become critical of them for minimizing these issues. Wives tend to bring up difficult issues because they want certain situations to change. They usually do this by nagging their mates. Men, in turn, feel pressure and withdraw even more. As couples do this,we have a ready-made formula for the pursuer/distancer dyad. Like so many of the couples, they are playing a "marital Pac-Man," where one chases the other in an effort to "chomp them up." Both resent each other for the patterns they have established.

When the wife gets upset, she may resort to whining, nagging, or criticism. Statements like "Why don't you…?" "Why can't you…?" "You never…," or "What's wrong with you?" fly out of her mouth. Unfortunately, this defeats her purpose because it creates in her husband the avoider reaction, which is the number-three predictor of divorce, known as *defensiveness*.

Defensiveness

As the Pursuer (often times the wife) becomes more reactive and begins to spout a litany of the wrongs in the marriage, her criticisms create defensiveness in her husband. As accusations are hurled, he becomes inflamed with the natural desire to defend himself. The more she hurls exaggerated details, the more defensive he becomes. He then starts to make excuses, lay blame, or develop some criticisms of his own. "I'm only doing this because of you," may bluster out of his mouth.

Criticism begets criticism, and defensiveness begets defensiveness. No one is truly being heard when this happens. Because each partner has been wounded, and attempts to heal these wounds have been unsuccessful, each person begins to build resentment and even unforgiveness toward his or her mate. Their souls no longer feel nourished and safe. Their needs are not being met as they once were. This leads to the last predictor of divorce, *contempt.*

Contempt

Research shows that it takes twenty positive comments to make up for one "zinger."[2] Because of this, you can see that couples who are in this criticism/defensiveness pattern are moving quickly downhill in terms of building a caring, warm relationship. Some even quit. They may quit literally, or emotionally, by having an affair or diving into television, work, or children. Either way, they are emotionally divorced. The pain of this behavior pattern causes contempt. All the passion and energy that once filled the relationship turns into a seething ember of hostility in their souls. This anger can move on the continuum from mere apathy—"I don't care. I'll just do my own thing and get my own needs met"—to pure hatred—"I cannot forgive my mate or trust him or her ever again." This bitterness and resentment can cause a couple to be overwhelmed with negative emotion. Because of this, they have a hard time seeing anything positive in the marriage at all. It can be very hard for a couple to reverse the negative effects of contempt.

As we studied Gottman's findings, we noticed that they looked very familiar to us. At first, we thought that we had read similar studies before, but upon looking further, we realized that all of the good doctor's findings can be found in the book of Proverbs. In our premarital counseling, our pastor said that there were enough proverbs to read one chapter a day for a month. He instructed us to do this through the first twelve months of our marriage so at the end of the year we would have read through it twelve times. We learned very early that the book of Proverbs is a virtual marriage manual for couples. There are so many verses there that relate to communication, problem solving, or relationships. Just take a look at a few.

- ◆ Stonewalling: Proverbs 24:26 says, "It is an honor to receive a frank reply" (TLB).
- ◆ Criticism: Proverbs 15:4 says, "Gentle words cause life and health; griping brings discouragement" (TLB).
- ◆ Defensiveness: Proverbs 11:29 says, "The fool who provokes his family to anger and resentment will finally have nothing worthwhile left" (TLB).
- ◆ Contempt: Proverbs 25:24 tells us, "It is better to live in a corner of an attic than in a beautiful home with a cranky, quarrelsome woman [or man]" (TLB).

Perhaps you and your spouse will want to do a word study of Proverbs, searching for information on healthy communication. You may want to use different versions of the Bible for increased insight. We often suggest that couples do this as a daily devotional, weekend Bible study, or for reading self-help material.

What happens to a couple who has slid down the slippery slope of marital dysfunction into contempt? It is hard for them to reverse their steps, so hard that Dr. Gottman often will not work with a couple in a state of contempt because he sees little hope that they can change. We say that if we did not work with contemptuous couples, then we would not have a job! The truth is that we work with couples in the state of contempt because we feel like we have a "secret weapon"—it is called the Holy Spirit. The Lord found us when we were contemptuous sinners and did not look away or find us hopeless. So we want to follow His example and give every couple a chance. The following is a story of one almost-hopeless case that moved from contempt to soul healing love.

Zach and Kelly's Story

Zach and Kelly came to our office as a last resort before filing for divorce. Kelly started the session by saying that she hated Zach for the things he had done in the marriage. "For starters," she said, "he has taken the family down his shaky vocational path for the last ten years. He has spent all the equity in our house on several stupid business ventures, and isn't even making much money in his business now. His irritability and temper have cut me to the quick all these years. But the final blow came when he told me he had had a brief affair with a girl at work."

"I keep trying to tell Kelly that my affair is over. It was a dumb mistake, and I will never do anything like that again," Zach retorted. "She just can't leave the past in the past. She's always gotta dig everything up and throw it in my face."

Already we see the pursuer/distancer dyad at work. Kelly would cry and then blow up and scream or magnify the problems in the marriage, while Zach would get defensive and minimize his transgressions. This created a vicious cycle that usually ended in highly destructive fights. While they both began to feel defeated, Kelly felt like quitting. Apathy took the place of angst, and eventually she began to feel hatred and contempt for Zach.

We see quite a few couples like Zach and Kelly. Sometimes we think that if they had only come in sooner, it might not be so bad. But often, we are one link in a chain of therapists who have attempted to get couples to heal their marriage, but to no avail. Our first task is to try to overcome their resistance to change.

Zach and Kelly's Resistance to Change

In the previous chapter, we showed you how a couple can get in touch with what is really eating them and why by completing the Digging Deeper Exercise. We shared this with Zach and Kelly, but they were so angry that they did not want to hear that the root of their anger was anything *but* their mate.

"What do you mean 'dig deeper'?" Kelly shrieked. "I don't have to dig any deeper than last month. You want to know the root of my anger? It's *Zach!* He's the cause of all this anger! It's all his fault. I don't have to dig any deeper to find that out!"

Zach, on the other hand, had a theory of his own. "You see what I gotta deal with here? She blames me for everything! The stinkin' car breaks down, and she's gotta say it's my fault. You want to know the root of my anger? You're lookin' at her!"

We knew from this that it would be a challenge for us to get these two to stop the blame game long enough to see what was really eating them, and what part they each played in their struggles. We started by inviting them to a Soul Healers Couple's Weekend. They were very skeptical, so we appealed to their budget. We made the point that the workshop was cheaper than paying an attorney a retainer for divorce proceedings. Besides, we told them, at least at the workshop you have a chance. Once you're in an attorney's office, you are on your way to the end. Finally, they agreed to come. We could now get them to take a deeper look at what their soul wounds were all about. Following are the results of the work they did.

Zach and Kelly's Digging Deeper Exercise

Step 1: We asked each person what their mate did that triggered their anger. Zach started first by saying that Kelly kept a long account of the wrongs he had done. He thought she would never forgive him, nor forget what he had done.

"I'm not saying that I was right in all that I did, but she will never let me live it down. I am afraid that she will make me pay for what I have done for the rest of my life! I just can't live this way! She uses this as an excuse to criticize me for everything that I do!"

We then asked Kelly to share her anger at Zach. She replied, "He is selfish and cares more for himself than for his family. He has taken us through a lot of shaky ground in regard to his many business ventures, and does not even care how I feel about things. I feel like his 'fling' was a personal slap in my face, after all my family and I have done for him!"

As we learned in the previous chapter, anger is not the primary feeling in a given situation. Underneath anger is a GIFT that will help set you free. Step 2 of this exercise was that both Zach and Kelly had to look at what was behind their rage.

Step 2: The GIFT Exercise. Remember the roots of anger are: **G**uilt, **I**nferiority, **F**ear, and **T**rauma (hurt or pain). We asked Zach, "How do you feel about this?" Zach took a moment and replied, "Sad, hurt, and never good enough for Kelly." In Zach's GIFT Exercise, he felt put down, and the roots of his anger were *Inferiority and Guilt.*

We then asked Kelly, "How do you feel about the way Zach treats you?"

She said, "Hurt and unimportant, like I am nothing to Zach, and like he could care less about me and the kids." In Kelly's GIFT Exercise, she felt the roots of her anger were *Hurt and Inferiority.*

Step 3: We asked each of them, "When in your (early) past have you felt this feeling before?"

Zach's Step 3: As Zach began to examine his past, he remembered that he had felt put down and hurt by his mother and father. He was the middle child of three boys, and his parents had very high expectations for all of them. When he was in junior high school, his grades slipped so they took him out of sports and made him study most evenings, while all of his friends and his brothers were playing on various teams. Zach had a difficult time with this because he loved sports and excelled there. He resented his parents for their lack of understanding. From that point, he began to rebel and get into trouble. He also never felt worthy enough or a part of anything after that. As an adult, he joined the military to try to find a place to belong, but it wasn't long before he rebelled against the strict structure and left after one term. He spent most of his adult life as a Christian trying to prove that he was good enough. This was the same kind of pain he felt when Kelly would put him down and criticize him.

Kelly's Step 3: Kelly grew up in a rural farm town in the southeast. She was the oldest of five children. Her parents were farmers, and the family always struggled for money. She started selling eggs and picking cotton for spending money when she was eleven. Unfortunately, most of the time, her dad would take her spending money without even asking in order to pay the family's bills. She tried to tell her dad how this hurt her, but he would shame her and make her feel guilty. All through her life, she carried a deep fear that she was not going to be provided for. When Zach would get one of his money-making ideas, she would feel that same fear again. When she would talk to him about it, he would minimize her fear or ignore it. With Zach, she felt the same hurt of the little girl who was responsible for taking care of her family amidst these hard times.

While Kelly described her father as a loving man, she said that when times were really hard, he would lose his temper and make her keep all of her siblings quiet or out of his hair so he could watch TV or go to bed. This feeling of pain and over-responsibility was exactly what she felt when Zach would have a "tantrum," as she called it, and tell her that he needed her help and support in order to be successful in his wacky business ventures.

After sharing this information and completing Steps 2 and 3 of this exercise, things began to shift for this couple. Kelly started to see Zach in a different light. He was no longer the insensitive, angry adult Zach who could care less about his family. Rather, she saw a young boy who felt he could never earn his family's love and approval. Zach did not see a critical, controlling adult Kelly, but rather, a frightened, hurt little girl who worried about her future and felt fearful of not having enough to get along. They started seeing a wounded child's face on each other.

Step 4: We asked them, "What do you do when you feel this way?"

Zach said, "When I feel inferior, like I can't do anything right, I'm not proud of myself, but I become passive-aggressive, or get angry and rage."

Kelly's response was, "When I feel afraid for the future, I try to control and fix everything. I do this by nagging or complaining."

It was a big step for them to be honest about their unhealthy coping mechanisms. It was clear that the very things that Zach did infuriated Kelly and only served to aggravate her nagging and controlling behaviors. Kelly's nagging and controlling response was just the behavior that sent Zach into a tailspin, where he was likely to become even more passive-aggressive (i.e., have an affair) or become angry and rage at Kelly. This, in turn, escalated their negative cycle. The principle of interactivity was now fully operational in their relationship, and they were deeply hurting each other. Remember, we tend to unconsciously select mates who will have similar wounds, but opposite adaptations, so their issues are interactive. It is easy to see why this couple would think that they were not good for each other. It is also easy to see why they would feel like giving up.

Step 5: We asked them the final question, "What do I really need?" Zach identified a lifelong need for approval and validation. He needed to finally feel good enough. His short-term need was for Kelly to "give him a chance," in other words, to try to forgive him and trust him again.

Kelly needed to feel provided for and protected by Zach. She wanted Zach not to rage at her. She also needed him to always be faithful.

It is important to note that many people list what they need in the negative like Kelly—that "Zach not rage at me anymore." Instead, we have them state their need in the positive because it is more effective in motivating human behavior. We encouraged Kelly to say—that "Zach love and cherish me, and act accordingly."

Motivating individuals by the positive, not the negative, has proven to be very effective in behavior modification and motivation theory. Have you ever heard a coach say to his best pitcher, "Whatever you do, don't throw an inside fast ball?" What do you think the pitcher does? You guessed it! He throws the most rapid inside fast ball of his career. Couples need to remember that motivating their spouse works better when they state requests in the positive, not the negative.

Our couple now knew what each other needed and why. They were just about ready to do the Behavior Change Request Exercise, designed specifically to change actual behaviors in each other. (This will be further explained in Chapter 10.) But even with the insight they received from the previous exercise, they were still blocked. They still saw each other in the enemy's camp. We knew we needed an extraordinary tool that would facilitate sharing and eventually forgiveness. It would have to be an exercise designed specifically for couples traveling in a very dark place in their relationship. So we put our heads together and developed the Forgiving Experience.

The Forgiving Experience

This exercise is based on a composite of several premises that we have learned through the last thirty years. The first is from Alcoholics Anonymous. We copied a form of their Fourth and Fifth Steps, in which individuals are encouraged to do a moral inventory of the wrongs they have done and begin the process of making amends for them. We have adapted this, however, to include a list of what your mate has done to you that you cannot seem to forgive, as well. The purpose of this is to, once and for all, clean the slate of past hurts and move the couple toward healing.

This is how it works:

Step 1: The offended partner, or the sender, asks for a time to share. The receiver, or the offender, grants the request as soon as they possibly can. Make sure you have about an hour when you can talk without being interrupted. (As you both get used to doing this exercise, either one of you may ask for a time to share.)

Step 2: The offended spouse, or the sender, shares all of the hurts and pains committed by their partner, much like a fourth-step inventory. As they do this, they give each offense all of the emotion that it deserves. They do this by incorporating the following rules: No tissue damage, property damage, or soul damage. This means that they can share how much pain they feel, but they cannot call names, threaten, or harm the other in any way.

This next part of the Forgiving Experience is based upon a technique called the *Container*, which is a part of Harville Hendrix's Imago Relationship Theory. He uses this tool to enable couples to express anger and resentment to each other in a safe and constructive environment.[3] One partner shares their anger about past wounds and hurts and the other serves as a "container" for their rage. During Step 2, the offender (receiver) listens with empathy and puts on his or her spiritual or psychic armor. They stay calm and focused as their partner's rage washes over them. This allows them to really hear what their mate is saying. There are two main purposes for this step in the exercise:

1. To say what hurts you, and give it the anger it deserves.
2. To once and for all, let the water "go under the bridge." In other words, let the anger be expressed and resolved so you can put the past in the past and move ahead in the relationship, unencumbered by past pain.

Step 3: The explosive phase is where the offended spouse (sender) externalizes their anger. They will talk about how angry they are and how that feels. The receiver, or the offender, listens with empathy and *koinonia*.

Step 4: The implosive phase is where the sender looks inward rather than outward and shares deep emotion and pain. They often cry and may even attach their current pain to some soul wound from their past. During this time of sharing deep emotion, the receiver still listens with empathy and *koinonia*. The offender (receiver) can provide support by hugging or touching their mate in a soothing way, but only if the sender desires this.

We have found that after the sharing of deep, internal, implosive emotion, couples take a natural pause or find a need for a break of some kind. It seems that giving a situation the anger it deserves can be very freeing for the soul. It tends to create a natural sense of "soul lightness" in the sender that is often accompanied by a sigh, a smile, or even laughter. We simply make this a part of the exercise. They can just take a deep breath, sigh, or simply catch their breath after sharing.

The next part of the Forgiving Experience is based on the work of the theologian and teacher, Lewis Smedes, in his work on forgiveness. In his book, *Forgive and Forget,* Smedes states that in order for true forgiveness to occur several things have to happen. One is empathy. The person asking for forgiveness must truly feel the pain that they have inflicted upon the other. The partner requesting forgiveness needs to be willing to empathize with their victim. This is not an easy task because it brings up all the guilt that the perpetrator does not want to feel.

Smedes also found that forgiveness is more likely to take place if the perpetrator, or in the case of this exercise, the receiver, makes a verbal confession or a statement of ownership of his or her hurtful actions.[4] This leads to **Step 5:** The receiver, or the offender, takes the lead and admits or confesses what he or she has done to hurt his or her mate.

Step 6: The offender furthers empathy and compassion by describing how the victim must have felt about the hurt he or she has caused. You might not know exactly how this hurt impacted your spouse, but developing empathy and compassion will help you put yourself in their shoes and feel what they felt.

You may have noticed that we have completed six steps of this eight-step exercise, and we have not allowed the offender to say he or she is sorry or beg for forgiveness. We delay this on purpose because offenders frequently offer apologies too quickly after an offense and do not give their souls time to develop genuine sorrow or true remorse. Offenders often do this to appease their terrible guilt. They then do not consider the humility and reverence that they need to request such a sacred act as forgiveness from someone whom they have wounded deeply. It is not until the seventh step that this is allowed.

In **Step 7**, the offender finally can reverently request his or her partner's forgiveness. A question is asked, perhaps something like, "Would you please forgive me?" or "Could you ever find it in your heart to forgive me?" We believe that forgiveness is a process and needs time. The offended person is not mandated to forgive immediately. We do not extort the offended partner to forgive immediately because we have seen a great deal of damage done by well-meaning Christians who guilt a person into forgiveness before they are ready. We simply encourage the offended mate to start the process of forgiveness with God's help as best they can at the time of the exercise.

We see too often that Christians wound each other, and then quickly ask for forgiveness. The person wanting forgiveness has little remorse, and the hurting person offers pardon out of guilt or duty, not from their heart and soul. Well call this forgiving without integrity. In order to truly forgive with integrity, both parties have to thoroughly consider the crime and give it the emotional and moral energy that is commensurate with it. The purpose of forgiveness is not only so that the requester can be pardoned, but also so that the victim can set his or her soul free. Unforgiveness is a poison to one's soul. Granting grace and absolution to a perpetrator frees one's soul. But it must be done with sacredness and a reverence that oft times can only come from God's supernatural power.

The last part of the Forgiving Experience is that of building trust. Couples often say that they are afraid to forgive because it means that the perpetrator can continue the hurtful behavior. This is one of the main reasons couples do not complete the forgiveness process. We instruct the offender to make a list of three to five key behaviors that he or she will commit to do that will build trust in the relationship. The offender then states the list in the form of a pledge of things that he or she will do. In this way, the statement is not just another empty promise that couples make after the heat of battle. It is a statement made with the full intent of one's heart and soul. At this point, the offender, or receiver, may not be able to guarantee that they can change completely, especially if they are dealing with an addiction of some kind, but they could guarantee their soul intent. Promising with one's heart and soul is a sacred covenant and cannot be taken lightly. This leads to **Step 8:** The perpetrator is asked to commit with the intent of his or her heart and soul never to wound his or her partner again. They then list the things that they pledge to do to win trust back in the relationship. This greatly aids in the healing process.

The eight steps of the Forgiving Experience may be the hardest eight steps a couple can take. But we have found that if the couple will ask for help in making them, they can actually heal the bitterness and contempt that causes their souls to spiritually and relationally atrophy. It is a sacred thing to be a part of a couple sharing from the depths of their souls. There is something awesome and completely reverent about being a catalyst for this kind of healing within a marriage. We felt this same reverence when Zach and Kelly shared their Forgiving Experience with us and would like to share it with you.

Zach and Kelly's Forgiving Experience

For our couple, Zach and Kelly, forgiveness was a very arduous process. They both had tremendous resistance, but they felt it might be their last hope. Kelly asked for a time to share, and Zach agreed and granted it as soon as he could, which is Step 1. Kelly listed all the soul-murdering offenses that Zach had committed against her in the marriage and how she felt about them. She started Step 2, the Explosive Stage, by telling Zach about her painful memories of his unemployed years and then moved into the other offenses. His response was to empathically put his psychic or spiritual armor on, and place himself in her shoes. He was to actually feel what it felt like to be Kelly experiencing these injustices. It took a good deal of prayer to help both Zach and Kelly with this process. Here is what they said.

Kelly: "I have never felt safe, protected, or loved by you. I lived in fear that you would go belly-up, and we would be on the street. You took too many chances with our money, especially when the kids were born." Kelly began to weep profusely. She was indeed giving it the anger and emotion it deserved.

"If I tried to tell you what was troubling me, you would get mad and yell, or pout and leave. I could never tell you how I felt without you making me pay somehow. Not only did I feel that I had to be responsible to pay the bills, and have some savings, but when I said no to some of your ideas, you would rage at me or punish me by closing me out. I hate you for that." At that point, Kelly cried very hard. Zach did his job as a "container," but several times he wanted to interrupt her, and he got defensive. We would calmly encourage him to keep his "psychic or spiritual armor" on, and just listen with empathy and *koinonia.*

Kelly continued, "The final blow came for me when you had a fling with that tramp at work. I just can't believe you would ever do that. I thought you would do a lot of things, but I never thought you would stoop that low! How could you do this to me? How could you break our trust? I am so mad and hurt at you that I could scream!" Kelly's voice was now very tight and angry, instead of tearful. She was fully into the Explosive Phase, but she honored Zach by not saying or doing anything damaging. "Zach, you almost killed me and destroyed us. What were you thinking? This makes me wonder if you ever loved me at all!"

Even though Kelly asked Zach questions, he was not free to answer them at this time because it would stop the flow of Kelly's sharing. As hard as it was for him, all he could do was listen with empathy.

She then began to connect her feelings about Zach to her painful feelings about growing up with her parents on the farm. At this point she moved into Step 4, the Implosion Phase. "I feel just like I did when I was a kid and had to sell eggs to help my family out. I felt then just like I do now, used and disregarded and that everything is all up to me." At this point, Kelly started weeping from her soul. "I felt all alone when I was a kid. I had too big of a burden to help the family survive. I hate feeling this way. I married you to be a helper, and I don't want to feel this way with you anymore. I'm tired, Zach. I can't take this kind of pain anymore." Kelly then did something interesting; she sighed a huge sigh of relief. I could tell she felt lighter just by the expression on her face. This created a natural pause so the couple could collect themselves.

We were now ready for Zach's part. He then needed to admit what he did and state it in a form of a confession (Step 5), and then make a statement of empathy to show Kelly that he could really relate to her feelings (Step 6).

Zach's Step 5: "Kelly, I see now how badly I hurt you when you supported me all those years going from job to job, and the thanks I gave you was to spend all of our money and cheat on you. I confess my awful behavior, and I feel terrible for hurting you so badly. You didn't deserve to be treated this way. You are right. I was only thinking of myself and not you or the kids. How could I do such a horrible thing to you?" Now Zach can make a statement of empathy showing that he has some idea of what Kelly must have felt.

Zach's Step 6: "Kelly, that must have been awfully scary for you all those years. You must have felt all the pressure was on you to take care of everything, just like you did as a little girl. I had no idea that so much was going on inside you. If I had to put myself in your shoes, I would feel so hurt and abandoned. You must be devastated inside." Zach spoke with great empathy.

Kelly started to cry again and whispered almost inaudibly, "Now you're finally getting it."

"I never meant to hurt you," Zach continued. "I did not do those things on purpose. I can't believe that I was so foolish and selfish. I can't believe I put you through so much pain and suffering. I really never meant to hurt you... I'm so sorry... I am so, so sorry..." A long pause took place. Zach looked at me and said, "I can't say it. I can't ask."

"What?" I asked him.

"How can I ask her to forgive me for all that I have done to her? I just don't feel like I could ever do enough to make it up to her."

"Now you are finally ready to ask your wife for forgiveness," I said.

It took a while for Zach to stop crying and collect himself. He was now ready for Step 7, which is requesting forgiveness. Finally Zach asked, with tears streaming down his face, "Could you ever find it in your heart to forgive me? Would you please forgive me?" There was a reverent pause before Kelly spoke.

Kelly: "Zach, I can't say that I can forgive you for everything yet. The affair... well, that's... that's just real hard. I can say that I will try with God's help to forgive you, but you've gotta try, too. You've gotta never do that stuff again."

Zach: "I won't." Zach waited for his cue from us to see what he was supposed to do next. "Kelly, I am so sorry that I put you through this. I don't want to lose you and the kids. Please believe me. I am so sorry." We then gently instructed him to make a commitment to the future to change his behavior. Zach had come prepared for this exercise, and he had made a list of all of the things he pledged to do to heal Kelly.

Zach's Step 8: "Kelly, I will ask my boss if I can stop traveling so much and to get me off the road. Until then, I will come home every day at 5:00 unless I'm dead. I promise to give the name and number of the hotel where I am staying if I absolutely have to travel. I will wear my beeper at all times, even to bed so you can always reach me. [This was before cell phones.] I will stay in individual therapy and couples therapy in order to understand myself and heal the pain I caused us. I promise I'll never be unfaithful to you again... never... never!" Zach said all of this as he quietly wept.

This is where God's awesome healing power takes over. This is where we as therapists feel that we are on holy ground. As Zach sat there crying in angst, his angry, hurting wife, his intimate enemy, the woman who declared absolute contempt for him, reached out gently and took his hand. This was the beginning of their peacemaking. They both looked into each other's eyes and started to cry, then spontaneously hugged each other as an outgrowth of the goodwill they felt at that moment. This is such a sacred time for couples that many times we just leave the room and let God's healing power engulf them. Even though we are the therapists and have seen this many times, with this couple we were crying, too.

This exercise was a real breakthrough for Zach and Kelly. It did not solve all of their problems, but it did redirect them onto a road toward healing. They rebuilt their relationship, and at the time of this writing, have been happily married for many years. They were blessed because many couples do not survive such indiscretions. We believe that the hard work they did developing empathy, genuine sorrow, and building trust in the Forgiving Experience enabled them to beat the odds against them and become soul healers. God bless you as you do this sacred work.

CHAPTER 10

IF NOTHING CHANGES, NOTHING CHANGES

*P*erhaps the hardest job of the therapist is to be a catalyst of behavior change. For most couples, the change process is much like Zach and Kelly's story. They fall in the same holes in the sidewalk of marital conflict over and over again and have a very difficult time getting out. Gaining insight into why you do what you do you can be very beneficial for many people. But if your dysfunctional behavior does not change, this insight can be seemingly useless. After all, change is what is desired in therapy, isn't it? Change is the main therapeutic bottom line. Couples want to know what is going to be different. They ask how their unhealthy behavior patterns can be altered. What can they expect to be modified? However, change can be very difficult for couples. In this chapter, we are going to examine couples' resistance to the change process, and what can be done about it.

Couples often come into the counseling process fraught with fear that the relationship will not be any different. This can create not only resistance to the change process, but can also sabotage any relationship modification, as well. Sometimes one partner may change, and the other does not even notice. Fear can blind a person to his or her mate's attempts toward healing. Many partners say, "I'll change only after my mate changes."

Neither mate wants to be vulnerable or take a risk until they see some goodwill gesture on behalf of their partner. These couples spend a great deal of time and energy in therapy resisting the change process, rather than working toward healing. They say things like:

> "He's been like this for thirty years. He'll never do anything different."
> "I'll have to do all the changing."
> "I changed, and she didn't even notice."
> "You can't teach an old husband new tricks. He is just set in his ways."
> "If I had money for every time I asked my mate to change, I'd be rich by now."
> "She'll change for a little while, but soon she'll go back to her old ways."

These are all statements made by couples. All of them are steeped in fear and pain, fear that the system will never change, and pain from soul wounds that life and marriage have inflicted upon them. Some of these couples have even stopped praying for their mate or their marriage. We see couples like these come in with all levels of hopelessness, from tiresome frustration or apathy, to actually living in an emotional divorce. Our goal is to bring about change, but first we have to rebuild the couple's faith.

Faith as a Resource for Change

Christian couples have the infinite resources of God Almighty at their fingertips, yet when they are afraid, they seem to forget this. Their fear and pain block God's healing power from reaching their souls. The daily grind of life and a difficult marriage cause it to fade from the horizon. These couples strongly desire their marriage to change, yet they continue in the same dysfunctional behaviors. Richard Stuart, father of Behavioral Marital Therapy, has a saying: "If nothing changes, nothing changes.[1]" This reminds us of the definition of *insan-*

ity: doing the same thing over and over again and expecting different results. This is, in fact, what most couples do. They repeat the same unhealthy patterns over and over again, while expecting things to be different. These couples can't forget that they have the power that created the universe at their disposal. They need to apply their faith in God's supernatural healing power to bring about behavior change in their marriages. They also need to take a look at their own behaviors, and if they are not working, change!

Resistance to Change

For couples to do this, they need to overcome the barriers or resistance to change. Motivational speaker Denis Waitley says that there are two basic human motivators—fear and desire.[2] These are the emotions that motivate people to change. We know that troubled couples have the desire to change or they would not be coming to counseling. We are then left with only one reason why they are not acting on their desire—their fear is too great.

In order to bring about change, we need to find out why the fear is there, and then begin to exorcise it. This fear manifests itself in several forms, all of which cause resistance to the change process. By sharing several of the reasons why couples resist change, we then can show people how to allow God's healing power to overcome their reluctance to become healthy. Following are some of those forms of fear.

Hurt

Many of the couples we see say they really want to live as soul mates. They hear sermons and Sunday school lectures on God's plan for intimacy between man and wife, but they are frustrated because they cannot seem to cultivate these fruits in their own life. Most of the time, their resistance is rooted in the hurt and pain that they have experienced in the past. These individuals feel so hurt that they cannot ever picture being friends, much less soul mates with their partner. Healing their hurt is essential if they are going to try to become soul healers.

Fear of the Unknown

There is a saying that "the devil you know may be better than the one you don't know." Even though their relationship may be unhealthy, some couples resist change because it is unknown. The familiar seems better than that which they have not yet experienced. The book of Exodus shows us the historical example of the children of Israel who would rather stay in captivity than risk the change that would bring about freedom. Their fear of the unknown held them back from the Lord's blessings. Many fearful couples can learn from their example.

Feeling Uncomfortable with or Unworthy of Happiness

Sometimes resistance to change can be traced to an unconscious feeling that you do not deserve to be happy. If you did not get your needs met as a child, or if your parents modeled an unhappy marriage, you may unconsciously feel like you should not have fulfillment or happiness, as well. This may not be an overt feeling, but you may have developed many covert ways to sabotage your marital satisfaction. You may unconsciously feel guilty if you are happy, and therefore find ways to ruin or sabotage it.

The exercises and tools in the Soul Healing Love Model have been proven to be very effective in healing many of these areas. They can also motivate you to move through your resistance to the change process. The Soul Healogram can show you if you have any unconscious feelings of guilt around being happily married. The Digging Deeper Exercise can show you any sabotage patterns that may cause you to resist behavior change. The Forgiving Exercise can help heal previous hurts you or your mate have inflicted upon each other, so you are both free to make the changes necessary to become soul healers.

This next exercise is designed specifically to heal problematic *behaviors*. The exercise comes from Behavioral Marital Therapy and has been used for years by behaviorists to help couples streamline the behavior change process. Harville Hendrix perfected it in the Imago Relationship Model, and it is a great way to get couples to bring simplicity and clarity to the change process so that change can be viewed as feasible and plausible. It is aptly named the *Behavior Change Request,* or BCR for short.[3]

Here is how it works. When frustration or anger occur in a relationship, you now have the Digging Deeper Exercise to help you attach your current situation to a soul wound and to determine the root feeling beneath your anger. From this technique, you are also able to clearly define your needs. You will notice from previous chapters that people define their needs in a very broad or general sense. We hear generalized statements like, "I just want him to love me more," or "I want her to respect me." While the goal is not stated in the negative, it is still much too broad. It is harder to accomplish goals that are too broad or too general. The more specific a goal is, the greater likelihood it can be achieved. Therefore, couples need to state their goals in very specific terms.

Dr. Harville Hendrix says that needs are more likely to be met if they are doable, measurable, and quantifiable.[4] *Doable* means that the goals are achievable or realistic. *Measurable* means that progress in meeting these goals can be ascertained, or that an estimate of what has been completed can be determined. And finally, *quantifiable* means that the quantity and frequency of the behaviors can be determined (i.e., when and how many times). The ability for couples to measure their progress helps them in the change process. It shows them their own progress, as well as their mate's. It also helps them see God's hand in the healing of their marriage. The Behavior Change Request provides couples with a tool to make behavioral goals more realistic, as well as achievable.

The Behavior Change Request (BCR)

To complete this exercise, you first need to state the needs you ascertained from the Digging Deeper Exercise. List each need on a sheet of paper entitled Behavior Change Request. Under each need, write three specific behaviors that will meet that need. For example, if you are angry and hurt with your spouse, and you complete the Digging Deeper Exercise and determine that you need more help and support from him, you will then need to list this need for help and support in the form of specific behaviors. Your BCR, or Behavior Change Request, would look like this:

Behavior Change Request

Needs:

Support and help with household chores.

Behaviors:

1. I would like for my mate to cook supper one night per week. This will start this week.
2. I would like for my mate to bathe the kids two nights per week. This will start next week.
3. I want my mate to listen to me talk about work, and later bring up various things that I have discussed. This will start this week.
4. I desire that my mate compliment my vocational abilities at least once every week. This will commence this week.

You can see that these goals are realistic and measurable. The frequency is specified so that they are quantifiable. There is also a starting time, which takes the anxiety out of wondering when one's mate will actually complete the desired requests. This also provides a means for the mate to "get credit" for the changes he or she has made.

Often one mate will make a few changes, but they will go unnoticed by their partner because there is no means by which to measure their progress. This can be very discouraging for the partner trying to change. It can even cause them to want to give up. The BCR takes the guesswork out of the couple's change process. It actually gives couples a roadmap to follow in healing their relationship.

"But Why Do I Have to Ask?"

Perhaps one of the greatest hurdles to overcome in completing the BCR is the feeling that the changes made are really shallow, phony, or contrived. Many people still believe the myth that "if someone really loves you, they can read your mind." Therefore they will know your need without your having to ask. We often hear things like:

> "If I have to spell out change, it is not from the heart."
> "Why do I have to tell him what I want and need? If he really loved me, he would just know."
> "She's only making these changes because I asked her to. Since it was not her idea, she doesn't mean it."
> "If I have to ask my husband to give me what I need, the gift loses its specialness."
> "My mate is only doing this because the therapist (mentor, lay counselor, pastor) said to do it."

All of these feelings are natural in the change process, but we have to face them head-on in order to overcome our objections to healing. Janet Woititz, in her book *Struggle for Intimacy*, says that one of the common false beliefs about intimacy is "if you really love me, you could read my mind."[5] There are several reasons for this false belief. One is the "love cocktail" that we learned about in Chapter Six. The biochemical high you receive when you fall in love creates an altered state of consciousness that often enables you to be totally tuned in to your mate. You hang on her every word. You finish his sentences. He rubs his head in pain, and you are there with two aspirin to remedy him. Your prospective spouse may grab her lower back and wince in pain, and you generously offer a backrub. You secretly find out that she likes a particular type of flower, and you put them on her front porch with a note that romantically intones, "Just because it is Tuesday." You and your partner do all of these things for each other without either of you having to ask. All of these behaviors lead you to the extremely misleading conclusion that your partner can read your mind. This is one of the reasons you love him or her so much. Getting your needs met, without even asking, is a wonderful blessing, especially if you grew up in a home where it was not all right to ask for anything.

You suffer from the delusion (or brain chemistry) that your partner is telepathic, knows your needs and strongly desires to meet them. So when the power struggle begins, when the honeymoon is over, you believe that he or she knows your needs but does not desire to meet them anymore. This is where you make up all sorts of motives about your partner:

> "He just does not love me enough to meet my needs."
> "She tricked me when we first met by being so caring in the beginning of our relationship. Then she started cooling off."
> "He is just a selfish jerk who cares more about himself than me and my needs."

None of these things are completely true. However, they are steeped in fantasy and delusion, just like the notion of your mate's marvelous mind-reading ability. The truth is that most people are not telepathic or psychic. They may get lucky with the help of certain brain chemicals, but they truly cannot read minds. The whole mind-reading notion can be put peacefully to rest if couples would just remember this premise: "The likelihood of your needs getting met increases proportionately with your ability to *ask for them out loud*." It has been substantiated through research on relationships that one's needs are met in proportion to one's asking.

"But What If I Don't Have Any Needs?"

There are two types of people who have trouble stating their needs. The first kind is what we refer to as the "needless." These individuals are usually in fields of study that require a well-developed left brain. They are extremely rational and logical and can be very unemotional. Because of this, they see themselves as very strong and rarely focus on their psyche or soul needs. These individuals usually choose professions that require a great deal of left-brain logic. They may be engineers, scientists, chemists, lawyers, or doctors.

Then there are those who have trouble sharing their needs because they have been trained not to do so. Many of them grew up in homes where they were told it was either wrong or selfish to share their needs. Some people's needs were merely ignored or unrecognized by their family, so they stopped stating them. These people have needs, but deny them. They ask for little in a relationship, but tend to expect their partners to give to them without their having to ask.

Darren and Samantha's Story

Darren was a trauma surgeon. He was used to putting his needs aside for the good of others. Working long hours in the ER with little sleep had become a way of life for him. Samantha was a writer for a local magazine. She was used to expressing herself, needs and all. They came into our office at Sam's initiative because she was not happy with their current situation. We asked them what they wanted to see different in their marriage. Sam, who was gifted with articulation and had a good command of words, eloquently and thoroughly listed six things right off:

"That Darren share more of his feelings with me."
"That Darren listen more to my feelings."
"That Darren show interest in reading my articles."
"That Darren spend more time with me and the kids."

"That Darren share his spiritual side with me, and listen to me share mine."

"That Darren and I become soul mates and share each other's internal world."

It was obvious that Samantha had no trouble being aware of her needs, feeling her needs, and sharing her needs. It is no surprise that she would be attracted to her opposite, Darren, who had only one need:

"That Samantha not have so many needs!"

They definitely had a problem in their relationship. To determine the root, we had to look deeper into Darren's life to see where he learned his self-denial and seeming needlessness.

Darren was raised in a loving Christian home. He described his parents as "pillars of the church." His dad was also a trauma surgeon and worked long hours. Dad was also a very active community servant and spent a week every year in medical service in a third-world country. Darren's dad was a loving and warm man, and an excellent example of selflessness.

Darren loved his dad and wanted to be just like him. I once asked him what he thought his dad wanted and needed most out of life. He was baffled. He did not have a clue. "My dad never had needs," he sighed. "At least he never shared them." At that moment the "idea light bulb" went off in Darren's head. He suddenly realized that he was following his father's example. He had repressed his needs just as his father had. His dad taught him well how to push his own needs down in order to attend to the needs of others. Darren feared that by sharing his needs, he would be perceived as selfish or self-absorbed. This realization was wonderful for him, because it allowed him to start recognizing what was really going on inside him.

Samantha lovingly and gently shared with Darren her excitement that he had finally recognized he had needs.

"For so long, I thought something was wrong with me," Samantha exclaimed. "I thought I was terribly needy and that Darren was the strong one. I never felt that he needed me for anything. For years he made me feel useless in our relationship."

Samantha warmly invited Darren to share his needs with her. She encouraged his vulnerability, and shared her own. As Darren began to state his wants and needs with his wife, the two became closer.

He was surprised and pleased as he shared, "What a paradox! I always thought that denying my needs would make me a noble and good husband. Now the wonderful truth is that by sharing that I have needs, I get a chance to heal myself, and my wife feels even closer to me than ever before. She actually likes me better this way!"

The bottom line is that Darren learned that it is normal to need. Once he began to share his needs with Sam, it was not so difficult for them to complete the Behavior Change Request Exercise. Now both Darren and Samantha could ask for and receive what they wanted in the marriage. Both were grateful for having the BCR as a tool to make this happen.

Mirroring, or Parroting

When you are doing a BCR Exercise, it is important to really listen to your mate's requests. In order to assure this, it is best to give your mate direct feedback, word for word. Some relational theorists call this process *mirroring*, while some call it *active listening*, or *parroting*.[6] No matter what term is used, the result is much like the mimic game we played as children to annoy our younger siblings and peers. I can still hear my younger brother's frustrated whine as he pleaded with me to stop repeating every word he said.

While this may have been annoying to you as a child, you will learn that it is very helpful for you as a grown married person. You will be surprised how you or your mate can have trouble listening to even simple requests and feeding them back.

Tom and I were in class to become Certified Imago Therapists, and our assignment was to pair up with a fellow classmate and mirror what they were saying. I must say that I did great! I mirrored their voice inflection, pitch, tone, body language, and even restated their phrases word for word. I thought I had really mastered this technique. Then it was my turn to mirror Tom. As he started sharing some of his frustrations with our marriage, I couldn't believe how hard it was for me to mirror him. I had trouble concentrating. I wanted to minimize or dismiss his concerns. I felt defensive and hurt and wanted to fight back or interrupt him. All of these reactions kept me from really hearing what he had to say. I was amazed at how hard it was to be a calm reflective mirror when my own reputation as a partner was at stake. Becoming a true mirror was very hard for me. The hotter the issue, the harder it was for me to truly reflect Tom's feelings. I realized then why mirroring is so important in the change process with couples. Without this tool, it is too hard for most couples to hear what their mate is saying, especially when it shines a negative light on themselves. This process of mirroring makes it possible for couples to hear each other and even show one another that they are doing so.

Steps 2 and 3 of the Behavior Change Request

Now we are ready for the next step of the BCR. Your mate states one of the three requests on his or her list and you repeat it back verbatim. In other words, you mirror their request. The only question you can ask is, "Did I get that right?" If you did not, then repeat the request until you do get it right. This may be hard at first, but give it time. You will both need to be patient because this will be new for you. Have your mate repeat all three requests, and follow the procedure for mirroring them. After each request is stated and mirrored, you may then agree to one, two, or all three of them. You will also state a time in which these requests can realistically be granted.

Let's say that your mate requests that you help more with the housework, and she suggests that you wash the dishes at least two nights per week. After you have mirrored this request, and you are sure you have heard your partner correctly, you then make an agreement to grant this request. Remember, you can only promise to do what is realistic in a timeframe that is plausible. If you are going to be traveling away from home all next week, that is not the time to grant this request. You will want to save this for a week when it can be properly granted. The goal is not to have couples make grandiose promises that cannot be fulfilled. While the intent may be noble, the followthrough may be deadly. Empty promises can cause even greater pain in an already stressed marital relationship. This needs to be avoided as much as possible.

When you agree to a request from your partner, you are simply granting these petitions with no strings attached. You are not making deals with your spouse, or worrying about what you are going to get out of this. You do not grant your mate's wishes so that he or she will grant yours. This is not a quid-pro-quo, or tit-for-tat interaction. The goal is not to give so you can get, nor to do for them so they can come through for you. Our goal is rather to give freely, with no ulterior motives. You give your mate a present.

The Giving of Presents

Webster says that a *present* is a thing that is furnished or endowed as a gift. This gift, or present, is given unconditionally. It is offered as absolute, not subject to any conditions on the part of the giver. What you give to your partner is really *agape*. Does this term sound familiar to you?

Agape, which was discussed earlier in this book, is the Greek term found in Scripture meaning benevolence or charity, undeserved favor. It is listed as the highest form of love. When given, it is not dependent upon the worth or value of the receiver. When expressed, it carries no obligation. *Agape* is favor given with no requirements or conditions.

Hendrix views *agape* as an act of directing *eros*, or life energy, away from ourselves and toward the welfare of another. It is sacrificial, but what is sacrificed is not self, but rather our preoccupation with self. *Agape* used as a noun denotes attitude, as a verb it denotes action towards another.[7]

Christ's Example of *Agape*

It is against our human nature to give unconditionally. We humans tend to give to get. The directive of Christ to love our enemies and bless those that hurt us, to turn the other cheek, goes against our very nature. How can we care for those who do not care about us? How indeed can we care for our mates when we perceive them as uncaring, or even enemies? This is where we need God's divine help. We need to call on His unconditionally loving nature to enable us to actualize that part of ourselves that is the most Christlike. Christ then becomes the inspiration for us to transcend our humanity and follow His example. The solution to our human condition in marriage is simple. It is to love our mate as Christ first loved us. Remember, it is simple, not easy. Even with Christ's loving example to guide us, it is still hard for most Christian couples to move beyond the typical deal-making, tit-for-tat marriages that we are so used to. To quote Hendrix:

Most marriages run like a commodities market with loving behaviors as the coin in trade. But this kind of love does not sit well with the old brain. If John rubs Martha's shoulders in hopes that she will let him spend the day going fishing, a built-in sensor in Martha's head goes, "Look out! Price tag attached... Unconsciously she rejects John's attentions and affections, because she knows that they were designed for his benefit, not hers."[8] The only kind of love the old brain will receive is the kind with no strings attached. This need for unconditional love comes straight from childhood. When we were infants, love came without a price tag. We did not have to reciprocate when we were patted, rocked, or fed. Now that we are adults, the old brain still craves this kind of unconditional giving. We want to be loved and cared about without doing anything in return. When our partners grant us caring loving behaviors regardless of what we do, we feel the familiar warmth, comfort, and security of our childhood.

By giving our partner presents, with no strings attached, we are healing not only their old brain, but also their soul wounds. We can give these presents freely because Christ freely gave His love to us. Thus, we give to our partner, because Christ gave Himself to us.

Agape in Action

For years as marital and family therapists, we worked with couples to help them gain insight and then make deals. We were both trained that if couples gained enough awareness and made enough trades, they would one day feel safe in marriage. We now believe that couples do not heal their souls by deal-making or insight. The wounds of soul are healed by *repetition*, the old brain experiencing presents, given repeatedly and consistently, as well as freely and unconditionally, by their partner. Repetition reprograms the old brain. We believe that is why daily prayer and Bible reading are so important for Christians. As believers, we need to be "programmed" daily to turn away from the old man, or sin nature. Couples need this same programming. They need to daily do things that will be healing for each other so that the soul wounds stored in the old brain can have time to heal.

The Coffee Story

We learned this valuable lesson after attending a couple's retreat several years ago. We were asked to make a list of things that our mate could do that would make us feel secure and loved. Richard Stuart in Behavioral Marital Therapy calls this developing "caring days," where couples take days in their relationship to show love and care for one another in order to make the atmosphere in the marriage more positive.[9] I (Bev) put on my list that I would feel warm and loved by Tom if he would serve me a cup of coffee in bed every morning when I woke up. This was particularly meaningful to me because I felt that I was not nurtured much in this way as a child. He gladly agreed, and diligently brought coffee to me every day for about a week. To be honest, I thought he was only bringing it because it was on my list. Not only did I doubt his sincerity, but I also doubted if he would continue. (See what kind of tricks your old brain can play on you?)

About two weeks after we started this process of giving unconditional presents to each other, we had a spat. Because of my (Tom's) hot Portuguese temper, I am sad to admit that when we went to bed, I *did* let the sun go down on our anger, against the Bible admonition. Bev used to ask me, "Does the sun ever go down in Portugal?" It was down, but I was still hotter than a firecracker.

When I awoke the next morning, I was still upset, and all I could think about was that cup of coffee. Even after my prayer time, I was still arguing with the Lord about whether or not I had to give Bev that coffee. In my mind, I rehearsed all of the unfairnesses and injustices that made her so unworthy of my present. I finally indignantly made a deal with the Almighty: *I'll give her the present, but I don't have to like it!* (Looking back, I see how ridiculous this was, not to mention, how ungodly.)

I got the coffee for her, stomped up stairs, sloshed it down on the nightstand by the bed and walked away piously. I patted myself on the back for acting intentionally and "faking it till I made it." It was so hard for me to act intentionally in the midst of my frustration and anger. Bev could tell I was frustrated because I spilled some of the coffee when I put it down. But when she saw the cup of coffee still sitting there amidst my anger and frustration, she was overwhelmed. She was so overcome with emotion that she started to weep from her gut. She was crying soul tears. I felt terrible and immediately ran in to apologize.

"I'm sorry if I damaged your nightstand. I can fix it," I consoled. I thought she was upset because I had messed up the furniture. "Please don't cry. It isn't that bad of a spill. We can clean it up."

"No," she said, gasping to catch her breath. It took a minute for her to compose herself because she was crying so hard. "I'm not crying about the nightstand, I'm crying because for the first time in my life since I can remember, someone was angry with me and still acted loving anyway. I'm crying because, even though you were frustrated and aggravated with me, you kept your promise to act lovingly toward me."

Bev and I had a few sacred moments of crying together, as we shared the awe and wonder of healing the old brain by the Giving of Presents. The tears that she shed were the tears of a child who finally felt unconditionally loved (*agaped*), no matter what. Our souls melted into each other, and we got a little closer by sharing that special time together. It has been several years since that day, and I (Bev) still get my soul healing cup of coffee every morning. This loving act has healed a great deal in me and reprogrammed my old brain of many traumas.

One interesting note is that the sense of smell or olfactory center of the brain is located the closest to the limbic system or old brain. This is why smells can very easily and quickly trigger old brain trauma. The interesting and wonderful thing about my soul healing cup of coffee is that now whenever I smell coffee (and with a coffeehouse on every corner, this is quite often), I am reminded of Tom's great sacrificial love for me. What a gift it is! How good God is to allow me this little bit of old brain healing every time I smell coffee!

We are still awed by this vivid example in our own marriage of the power of the Giving of Presents in the healing of our old brain, as well as our souls. As you, with God's help, agree to give presents to your mate, you can truly become a soul healer.

The Giving of Presents Exercise

In order to complete this exercise, each of you needs to make a list of behaviors that would express *agape* to you. The list would read as follows:

I feel warm and loved by you when you...

You then fill in the list with soul presents that you would like to receive. You and your mate exchange your lists, and you each pick one present that you are willing to bestow upon your spouse within a three-day period. The lists can be updated regularly. Remember, this is not a time to extort or test your partner. Don't list things like "move away from your in-laws," or "buy a bigger house." These are soul healing presents we are talking about here, not deals to be made or "proof" of love. One further note: It is imperative that the presents be given consistently and as soon as possible. Do not resolve to give a present if you know you can't or won't follow through. It would have been even more damaging to my soul if Tom had brought me coffee for several weeks and then faded in his efforts. The Giving of Presents is a sacred covenant that must be done consistently and reverently.

Putting It All Together—The Behavior Change Request

In closing this chapter, we will put all the steps of the **BCR** together so that you can see, from start to finish, how to complete this exercise.

Step 1: Identify your need. Use the Digging Deeper Exercise if you need to.

Step 2: State your needs in the form of three behavioral requests. Make sure the requests are doable, measurable, and quantifiable. Give a starting date.

Step 3: Your mate mirrors or repeats each request, asking only if his or her mirror is accurate: "Did I get that right?" or "Is there more you want to say?"

Step 4: Your partner agrees to one, two, or all three of the requests, stating the time that they will be completed.

Step 5: You and your mate consistently follow through on your partner's requests.

In this chapter, we have seen that the consistent, sacred, unconditional giving of soul healing presents can heal the old brain and form a lasting bond between husbands and wives. This act of giving soul healing presents replicates God's unconditional love for us. This idea of *agape* is really His idea and His design for couples. The next chapter discusses in detail what God has in mind for a Christian marriage.

CHAPTER 11

SOUL HEALING LOVE IS GOD'S IDEA

We see so many couples in counseling that merely exist in their marriages. Some have tasted a small sampling of soul healing love during the romantic stage of their marriage, only to quickly watch it fade away as they slide full force into the power struggle. Some even less fortunate couples have actually forgotten any semblance of the chemistry, passion, and caring that brought them together in the first place. In the previous chapters of this text, we have tried to share remedies to these relational maladies. But perhaps one of the biggest obstacles we have to overcome in the healing of relationships is the false belief by many people that soul healing love does not really exist. These lonely travelers on the road of relationships have all but given up on finding the love of their lives. Here are a few examples of these weary travelers.

Herman, the Not-So-Confirmed Bachelor

There was Herman, a thirty-nine-year-old rich, handsome bachelor, who came to see us because he wondered if he would ever find the "perfect girl." He had dated supermodels and corporate executives who made six-figure incomes, and still he became disillusioned about finding his soul mate. We told him the problem was not that he had failed to find his soul mate; the problem was that he had not found the "soul mater" within him. He had not yet learned to love with a soul healing love. Learning to love in this fashion is not a mystical ability; it is a skill that is to be ascertained, honed, and practiced.

"You mean that I haven't overlooked my soul mate? You mean she may still be out there somewhere? Do you think it's possible that she hasn't married somebody else, and had three kids by now?" Herman blurted out.

"No, indeed," we told him, "your soul mate will appear when you have learned to become a soul healing partner. What has been missing in your past relationships is *you*."

Herman's quest for the perfect soul mate "out there some-where" kept him from learning the skills he needed within himself to be a soul healing lover.

Oliver and Lisa, the Married Skeptics

Oliver and his wife of six years, Lisa, were told by family and friends that marriage was to be endured, and that that was all one could expect from matrimony. Lisa wanted more. She wanted a soul mate. People told her that this did not exist. Her grandmother told her she could expect some of this soul mate "nonsense" during the courtship (maybe Grandma knew a little about phenylethylamine), but once the honeymoon was over, she told Lisa that she would just have to "settle for what she got!" To top this off, Grandma added, "And it is God's will that you never divorce!" This left Lisa and Oliver feeling more like they were sentenced to a jail term than committing to matri-mony. Lisa was particularly disillusioned at the notion of making do in marriage. She had almost given up hope that true soul healing love was possible, until she heard us speak at her church. Our lessons gave Lisa some hope, but Oliver still remained a skeptic.

"This soul healing stuff just isn't for me," he'd tell Lisa, re-fusing to attend a couple's retreat, much less darken the doors of a counseling office. "Who says this really even exists?" he would lament.

Lisa tried numerous times to convince Oliver that this kind of love was possible. He would adamantly resist her attempts. She started feeling as if she was putting Oliver through too much. She worried that she was being almost cruel to him by trying to change him to meet her needs.

"Isn't this too much to ask of your mate?" she would question. "What if I just picked a man who cannot do this? What if I am asking Oliver to do something that is impossible for him? What if I picked the wrong mate and my soul mate is still out there somewhere?"

It did not help her angst and guilt when Oliver acted like Lisa was torturing him by asking him to come to marriage counseling. What Lisa did not realize was that she would not be hurting or tormenting Oliver, she would actually be healing him by asking him to change. Oliver, like all humans, was created by God to be a soul mate. God intended for all of us to build oneness of souls with another human being. God's plan is that we find a lifetime partner and learn to merge our souls with their's. This union creates a soul healing bond. Every soul needs this healing. Every soul needs to learn to love in this manner. By acquiring this awesome ability, we are actualizing our full spiritual potential, which makes the heart of God dance. God's love for each of us heals our souls, and God wants us to replicate this kind of love with our lifetime partner. By doing this, we will become more Christlike, which is the aim of all Christians. God created all of His children to love and be loved, even Oliver.

Each time Lisa would ask Oliver to come to counseling with her, he would vehemently refuse, but then she would notice that he would act better toward her. He would come home earlier, send her flowers, or offer to do the dishes. He thought that this would change Lisa's opinion that their marriage needed help. Later, when she would bring up counseling again, he would become defensive and shout, "I can't believe that you still want to see a counselor, after all the changes I have made! You just want too much. I can never do enough for you! Why do you keep trying to change me?" Oliver's fear and resistance to change was overtaking him. He, like many Christians, thought counseling was for crazy couples who yelled and screamed and hated each other. He told Lisa repeatedly, "I don't see why two perfectly healthy Christian adults cannot work out their problems on their own." We have heard this prideful attitude from Christians so many times. The sad thing is that while this pride may prohibit them from going to a counselor's office, this same pride just may carry or even push them into the divorce attorney's office. This is such a sad plight for Christian couples.

Our goal quickly became to coach Lisa on how to get Oliver to come to marriage counseling. We encouraged her to share this story with him:

> If you had a cyst on your arm that was full of germs, you could go to the drugstore and buy some Bactine and a bandage and apply it to the lump, in hopes that the infection would abate. It may go away with this course of treatment, but in all likelihood, the germs will exacerbate, and the cyst will begin to swell even more. When this happens, you will feel pain. You could choose to apply your familiar Bactine again, but the wiser choice would be to see a doctor. If you resist seeing a professional, the infection could become acute, and you may even stand to lose your arm.

This is what you, Oliver (and many other resistive spouses), are doing when you try to cure the infection of your marital problems with the simple Bactine of bettering surface behaviors. Your marriage needs the antibiotic of marriage counseling. You need a marriage doctor. You may even need to lance that matrimonial commitment, so the pus of negative energy and contempt can drain properly. Resisting the help that is available could be deadly for you and your marriage.

The story worked, and Oliver agreed to come to marriage counseling. It took a while for him to overcome the feeling that he was being tortured by having to learn to be a more feeling person. He and Lisa came to a Soul Healers Workshop and then joined a Soul Healers Couples Bible study at their church. In time, Oliver began to believe that soul healing love was possible. He even started to see that it wasn't torment or punishment for the average testosterone-laden male to learn to share his feelings and become a good communicator and listener. They even attended an Advanced Soul Healers Workshop, and Oliver blessed us all by openly thanking his wife for pushing him to come to marriage counseling.

We all cried as he tearfully shared: "No one was more resistant to coming to counseling than me. I was a true skeptic. I equated marriage counseling with having a root canal! I had no desire whatsoever to look at my childhood. I guess I was just scared. I have had a change of heart, however, and I want to thank my wife for fussing, begging, pushing, and pulling me to come." (At this point, Oliver could not hold back his tears, nor could we.) "In my whole life, I never thought that this kind of love was possible. I guess it was because my parents have been in a miserable marriage for forty-five years. But things are different now. My wife is my best friend, and our relationship just keeps getting better and better. I want to say to all the husbands in the group that you can have this, too. Thanks, honey, for not giving up on me. Thanks, Drs. Bev and Tom, for being our marital tour guides and for teaching us the tools of soul healing love. I feel like all of the hard work has been worth it."

Imagine all of this from a guy who initially refused to come to counseling! Oliver was and is one of our best advertisements for soul healing love. He still sends his friends, family, and church members to our office for counseling. As you can see, Oliver and Lisa's growth had a precious, sacred impact on us all.

The Thread of Love

So, how do we achieve this soul healing love? Let's look at the various types or meanings of love as a clue to the single thread that runs through our marriage. When couples meet, they feel *eros*, or romantic love. We have shown you that this love is delusional and has a very self-indulgent quality. The theories of *Chemistry*, *Imago*, and *Projection* in Chapter Six reveal that you are attracted to someone who makes you feel good about yourself. Thus, you love someone because they can meet your needs. In actuality, you love them because of what they can do for you. Since your needs are met, you have a false sense of euphoria, thus you are more willing to meet the needs of your partner. However, this motivation is still somewhat selfish and self-serving.

As the power struggle starts, and your needs are not being met, you do not feel like giving. You even want to withhold and sometimes seek revenge or retaliation for the pain you feel. It is then that you must practice unconditional, undeserved favor and love. It is when you least feel like it that you need to extend *agape* to your partner.

I once heard this saying: "In order to be truly safe, you must insure the safety of your enemies." Harville Hendrix amplified this by saying: "True peace—that is, peace without fear—exists only among friends. Peace with fear can exist between foes, but is *always* unstable!"[1]

In order to insure peace and safety between you and your partner, you must be willing to insure the peace and safety of each other. Because the power struggle has made you enemies, this peace will indeed be unstable. To bring stability to your relationship, you both must be willing to extend *agape* to each other. By giving your partner undeserved favor, you are extending the hand of friendship to your enemy. This act of goodwill causes a bond of friendship to form. Thus *philia*, or friendship, is born in your relationship. You and your spouse become friends.

The sequence of love moves from *eros* to *agape* to *philia*. You fall in love with delusional *eros* driving you, and become intimate enemies, because of your own human nature and power struggles. Then, as an act of your will, you learn to give *agape*, and gradually you and your spouse become friends. So, is this where love arrives? Is this the culmination of love in long-term marriage—friendship—*philia*? Wow, what a simple, not-so-exciting goal!

At first we, as therapists, were disappointed that love's destiny ended so simply and in such a seemingly commonplace way. Our confusion and disappointment led us to interview couples who had been happily married for over forty years to find out what they would consider as the primary advantage or benefit of long-term love. We were surprised at what we found. Without exception, all of the couples pointed to friendship. In one way or another, comments indicated friendship to be the key to fulfillment in a long-term healthy love relationship. Tom and I were expecting something more exciting like passion, mind-melding, or mutual spiritual nirvana. Instead, we heard that pure and simple friendship (*philia*) was the key. Here is a sampling of what they said:

From Greg and Vera, married forty-two years: "She is my best friend, and I would never do anything to hurt her." "I care so much for him; if he hurts, I hurt, too."

From Linda and Richard, married forty-five years: "We care for one another... We really care how the other one is feeling."

From Al and Murial, married forty-seven years: "The best advice we can give to young couples is, 'Be ye kind one to another.'"

From Robert and Mary, married fifty-seven years: "I can't imagine life without him. He is one of the few true friends I have." "I wouldn't take anything for the friendship we have developed over our lifetime. We are truly blessed."

From Virgie and Harland, married sixty years: "She is my companion and my best friend in the whole world. I am so grateful to God for giving her to me."

I still remember talking with this pleasant couple about their marriage. As we were sharing, Harland left the room for a moment. Without blinking, Virgie said, "Bring me one, too."

"Bring me one what?" Tom asked. Before Virgie could answer us, Harland walked in the room with two glasses of iced tea. "Here you are, darlin'. Your tea, just like you asked for it."

"Thank you, dear," she replied sweetly.

"Wait a minute," Tom said to Harland. "Vergie didn't ask for anything. How did you know what she wanted? She just said, 'Bring me one, too,' as you left the room."

They both looked at us somewhat puzzled, and Harland asked, "Didn't she ask for that tea? I could have sworn she asked."

"No," Tom said, "she didn't say a word."

As they both began to chuckle, Harland calmly replied, "Oh well, I guess we were reading each other's minds again! We do this all this time now. We communicate so well, I guess we forget to use words." Harland continued, "We tell our grown kids that this mind-reading stuff doesn't come easy. They've got to learn it like Mom and I did. We didn't always know what each other wanted. We had to get it by watchin' and just bein' around each other. We got it by carin'. You just can't start off like this; it takes years to develop." We felt privileged to be a part of that sacred moment between these long-term soul healers. It gave us hope for the future of marriage in today's times.

What we heard in our interviews is validated in Lauer and Lauer's article in *Psychology Today* entitled "Marriages Made to Last," which gives the results of a research project of happy couples in which the item ranked first by all couples was, "We are each other's best friend." The result of the study showed that friendship was the most significant factor in healthy, happy, long-term couples, winning over mutual political beliefs, similar financial styles, passion, and sexual fulfillment.[2]

To attain this friendship, we humans have to override our natural selfish instincts, and give *agape* in order to be friends. Most of us just cannot do this by ourselves. Our flesh gets in the way. How can we give to someone who makes us feel unsafe? How can we give to our enemies? This concept of giving *agape* to establish *philia* is just too much for mere mortals to comprehend. What could possibly motivate us to give this soul healing love to our perceived enemy? The answer is simple but not easy: We give unconditional love because we are first loved by God.

In Christ, We Are Loved, Lovable, and Loving

First John 4:7–11 says, "Beloved, let us love one another, for love is of God; and everyone who loves is born of God and knows God. He who does not love does not know God, for God is love. In this the love of God was manifested toward us, that God has sent His only begotten Son into the world, that we might live through Him. In this is love, not that we loved God, but that He loved us and sent His Son to be the propitiation for our sins. Beloved, if God so loved us, we also ought to love one another" (NKJV).

Matthew 22:39 says, "You shall love your neighbor as yourself" (NKJV).

Maybe that is the problem: We love our spouses like we love (or do not love) ourselves. If we do not love ourselves, then how are we going to love our partners? If we do not feel loved or lovable, then how are we going to be loving? We felt the Lord gave us the answer to this question one day as we were spending time with our own children.

We were watching our daughters play, as many doting parents do. We were amazed that God would give us two such wonderful and beautiful gifts. As we stared at them, we began to look for similarities between them and ourselves.

"Amanda has your hands," I said to Tom. "Nicole has your eyes and hair. She looks just like you did in your baby pictures."

"Nicole is the 'spitting image' of you, personality-wise," Tom said to me. "She has your smile."

Then it hit us. Our children were created in our image, and we cannot help but love them! Likewise, then, we are created in God's image, and He cannot help but love us! We are lovable, because God loves simple little humans like us. The idea that the Creator of the universe loves us unconditionally, without our striving to earn it, caused us to choke up right there on the playground. As we softly wept there together, we felt the warmth of God's love all around us. We felt worthy. We felt valuable. We felt lovable. The awesome power of this lovability enables us to love, or *agape*, each other. Thus we can offer unconditional love to our undeserving partner, because God first gave it to us. This unmerited *agape* from God fills us up. It is out of this fullness that we can give to our mate.

The Endless Cycle of Giving and Receiving

As God's children, you give because Christ Jesus first gave to you, just like the Scripture says. You do not have to rely on your weak human abilities to heal your marriage. You now have the power of your Lord to help you. It is by the Lord's power that your selfish human nature can extend *agape* to your partner. As your mate receives your love and feels its undeserved merit and favor, he or she feels propelled to reciprocate by giving *agape* to you. This creates an endless cycle of giving and receiving.

We found this to be true in our own marriage. When we first met, *eros* was hard at work. We had a great deal of chemistry and attraction nudging us. This created a desire in us to give to each other. We wanted to meet each other's needs. We did so spontaneously, without thought of what we were getting out of it for ourselves. When the power struggle hit, we were devastated. Our loving partner and friend, whom we had equated as close to Jesus, had now become Lucifer incarnate! Our good and trusted friend was now our foe! This was particularly difficult for us, because we had grown up in such dysfunctional homes. We counted on our marriage to be a place of healing for us, not further abuse. Our desire to give withered, as our pain and hurt grew. We loved each other, but we were becoming distant, untrusting, unsafe, and uncaring. We became intimate enemies. It was God's grace and our commitment to a Christian marriage that kept us looking for ways to bridge the gap between us. Even we, as marriage counselors, thought all the things that couples think in this despair:

> "He just doesn't care anymore."
> "She just wants things her way."
> "This situation is hopeless! He'll never change."
> "She's been that way for years. What makes me think she'll be different now?"
> "Maybe I just want too much."
> "Maybe you just want too much."
> "Is there something wrong with me?"
> "Is there something wrong with you?"
> "Maybe I just married the wrong person."

Amidst all of the frustrations of our marital power struggle, we did not stop searching for healing and happiness. At times we wondered about our determined quest for soul healing oneness. We wondered if we just kept up the search because we are so stubborn by nature. Maybe it was because we had been marriage counselors for so long, and we had learned to believe in this healing process. Maybe we were just a romantic optimists and liked old movies that ended happily ever after. Actually, our searching was a result of the healing that God had already done in our lives.

Here I (Bev) was, with a childhood history of physical, verbal, mental, and emotional abuse. I remember taking a class on the Abnormal Family in graduate school and finding that I had all twelve dysfunctions we learned about in my immediate and extended family. I should have been a candidate for a mental institution, not for matrimonial bliss. But despite all the pain and hurt I suffered at the hands of my earthly caretakers, I felt God's hand reach out to me and bring supernatural healing to my life. As a pathetic, hillbilly child with a negative self-esteem, and a family with a history of extreme dysfunction, there were many times when I thought life was not worth living. These suicidal urgings are not uncommon for adult children of dysfunction. These hopeless feelings stayed with me until I became a Christian.

Christianity brought healing and hope to my wounded soul. It was this healing that propelled my quest for the healing of the soul of my marriage, and other marriages like it. It was this search that led me to the door of the Creator and Originator of marital oneness. I found the solution to my dilemma at the feet of the Great Physician, the Omnipotent Marriage Counselor, the Author and Example of Oneness—Jesus Christ. I realized that Christ had already shown us how to do marriage. His relationship with us is our example of matrimony. He loves us with *eros*, not romantic love, but the more rudimentary definition—life energy.

Christ's love for us gives us life breath, or life force. This life force provides us with a clear purpose for our existence. However, our sinful nature causes us to fall short, and we disappoint Him. Instead of withdrawing or punishing us, He extends His loving hand of *agape* to us. His unconditional love for us builds a bond of friendship, or *philia*, between Jesus and His children. Being regarded and treated as the Lord's friend heals our souls and moves us toward our original life force, or life energy. Thus, we recapture our original *eros*.

We move from:

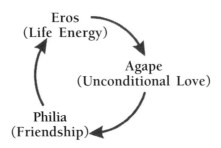

This is also what God intended for us as married couples. We are attracted to our partners because of our unconscious mating processes and instincts (see Chapter Six). These mating rituals are fueled by our need for life energy, or *eros*. Finding our life energy motivates us to give to our partner. When times get hard in a marriage (and they will), this life energy, or *eros*, fades from the repeated washings in hurt and pain. This is when *agape* becomes necessary. It is Jesus, the Author of *agape*, who gives couples the strength they need to unconditionally love each other.

From this love, the bond of friendship, or *philia*, is built. Couples become friends and commit to heal each other's soul. The energy that comes from this *philia*, or friendship, moves the soul back toward its authentic wholeness, back to its life force, or life energy, back to *eros* where it started. As a couple, we move from *eros* (life energy) to *agape* (unconditional love) to *philia* (friendship) and then back to our original *eros*.

Our marital journey follows the path that the Lord has traveled as our example. We move from:

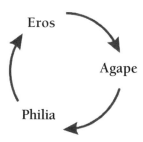

Yes, you return to *eros*, complete with positive energy, affection, care, and even some romance. You may even recapture some of the original passion and spark that was so much a part of your courtship. Your heart may partially skip a beat when your long-term mate enters the room. You may briefly become weak-kneed when you see your partner in a crowded shopping mall. You might play together and act like kids again. It is possible that you can rediscover why you fell in love in the first place so many years ago.

From reading the previous chapters, you see that phenylethylamine is released when people fall in love. But as you also learned, studies show that the continued presence of a long-term partner gradually steps up the production of endorphins in the brain. Unlike those crazy, hyped amphetamines, these are soothing chemicals, natural painkillers similar to narcotics. These endorphins give long-term partners a sense of security, peace, and calm. Thus, couples move from early love, fueled by amphetamines, to mature love that is laced with pleasant mellow narcotics.

Couples go from loving someone for what he or she can do for them, to loving someone for who he or she really is. They move from selfishness to giving, from narcissism to altruism, from passion to compassion, from falling in love to deciding to love. The result is that you have a partner to accompany you on your journey through life. You have a companion who knows and cares about your soul pain, and you have, and have become a soul healer. This, after all, is what marriage is all about.

EPILOGUE

With bells ringing and happiness of heart,
Our new life together was about to start.
It was all so new, an exciting dream,
But with all the changes, it never seemed—-
We would learn to love each other as we should.

Being married wasn't easy, so many people said.
A lot of people quit, but we worked at it instead.
We hardly made it through those difficult beginning years.
Our only consolation was that the Lord knew all our fears.
After having it so hard, I recollect in tears—
That maybe now, we can learn to love as we should.

We could hardly wait for our baby to arrive.
It seemed so hard to see that our love was now alive.
She brought us so much joy and happiness to share.
I can't tell you what it meant to me, just having you there.
Maybe now we can dare—
To love each other as we should.

With the busy life of diapers, and all the care a baby takes,
Sometimes our "couple time" was difficult to make.
The laundry, the bottles, the four A.M. feedings,
And many times our eyes were so desperately pleading—
For us to love each other as we should.

But there was tap and ballet,
And another child on the way,
And gradually more and more duties filled our day.
So sometimes we ignored what each other had to say.
And that made it even harder—
To love each other as we should.

We sat with each other through fevers and such.
I never really told you I appreciated it so much.
Your support meant so much to me; I often used it as a crutch.
If only we had time to allow our hearts to touch—
Then maybe we could learn to love each other as we should.

It seems like only yesterday, our precious gems were small.
I can't believe they're married, and they don't even call.
But the quietness in our home is the worst pain of all—
Maybe now we can learn to love each other as we should.

But your job went sour, and that caused you so much pain.
You gave so much to them, and there was nothing you
could gain.
I felt so useless in helping you,
I thought you'd never be the same—
Now I know we need to learn to love each other as we should.

Growing older isn't easy. No one warned us of the woes.
The moans, the aches, the groans, the sags,
Always keep us on or off our toes.
"We're not getting any younger,"
Isn't that how the old song goes?
Now maybe we will have the time—
To love each other as we should.

I can't believe it's you, lying there in that hospital bed.
After all the things we vowed, after all the things we said.
I was just learning to love you,

And now they say you're dead—
O God! Why didn't we learn to love each other as we should?

If I had to do it over, I'd love you more in every way.
I'd give to you, not think of me, and put my concerns away.
But a lonely tombstone has nothing left to say,
So I come here tearfully each and every day—
Praying to the Lord that you will forgive me
For never taking the time to learn to love you as I should.

The journey to becoming a soul healer is an exciting one; please don't wait. May God richly bless you as you embark.

Notes

Chapter 1

1. *Webster's College Dictionary*, (New York: Random House, 1995), see *synergy*.

Chapter 2

1. *Webster's College Dictionary*, (New York: Random House, 1995), see *soul*.

2. *Grolier's Encyclopedia*, [CD Rom] (Electronic Publishing, 1993), see *soul*.

3. W. E. Vines Expository Dictionary of New Testament Words (McLean, VA.: MacDonald Publishing Company), see *soul*.

4. John and Paula Sanford, *The Transformation of the Inner Man* (New York: Bridge Publishers, 1982).

5. Thomas Moore, *The Care of the Soul* (New York: Harper Perennial, 1995), xiii.

6. Ibid., xv.

7. Ibid., 17.

8. Harville Hendrix, *Getting the Love You Want* (New York: Harper Perennial, 1988), 35-37.

9. Harry Harlow, *Learning to Love* (New York: Jason Aronson, 1974).

10. Hendrix.,50.

Chapter 3

1. Larry Crabb, *Inside Out* (Colorado Springs: NavPress, 1988).

2. Paul Brand, "The Gift of Pain," *Christianity Today 17:1* (January 10, 1994) : 18.

3. Patricia Love, "Imago Therapy Certification Training Session," Lake Lure, NC, 1993

4. David Seamands, *Healing Damaged Emotions* (Wheaton: Victor Books, 1981).

5. Patricia Love, *"The Emotional Incest Syndrome: When a Parents Love Rules Your Life* (New York: Bantam Books, 1990).

6. Ivan BoszormeNyi-Nag and Geraldine Sparks, *Invisible Loyalties* (New York: Brunner Mazel, 1983).

Chapter 4

1. Robert Ornstein and David Sobel, *The Healing Brain* (New York: Simon Schuster, 1987).

2. Harville Hendrix, *Keeping the Love You Find* (New York: Pocket Books, 1992), 41.

3. Patricia Love, "Imago Therapy Certification Training Session," Lake Lure, NC, 1993

Chapter 5

1. Thomas Moore, *Care of the Soul* (New York: Harper Perennial, 1994).

2. Ibid., 53.

Chapter 6

1. Anastasia Toufexis, "The Right Chemistry," *Time*, February 5, 1993, 48

2. Neil Clark Warren, *Finding the Love of Your Life: Ten Principles for Choosing the Right Marriage Partner* (New York: Pocket Books, 1992), 83.

3. Ibid., 81.

4. Harville Hendrix, *Keeping the Love You Find* (New York: Pocket Books, 1992), 21.

5. Ibid., 162.

6. Dorothy Tennov, *Love and Limerance: The Experience of Being in Love* (New York: Stein & Day, 1970), 117.

7. Patricia Love, *The Truth About Love* (New York: Simon Schuster, 2001), 29.

8. John Sanford, *The Invisible Partners* (New York: Paulist Press, 1980), 18.

Chapter 7

1. Patricia Love, "Imago Therapy Certification Training Session," Lake Lure, NC, 1993

2. Harville Hendrix, *Getting the Love You Want* (New York: Harper Perennial, 1988), 81.

3. Beverly and Tom Rogers, *Adult Children of Divorced Parents: Making Your Marriage Work* (San Jose: Resource Publications Inc., 2002) 82.

Chapter 8

1. *Webster's College Dictionary*, (New York: Random House, 1995), see *projection*.

Chapter 9

1. John Gottman, *The Marriage Clinic* (New York: W. W. Norton, 1999).

2. Pat Springle, Close Enough to Care (Dallas: Ralph/Word, 1990), 184.

3. Harville Hendrix, *Getting the Love You Want* (New York: Harper Perennial, 1988), 170.

4. Lewis Smedes, Forgive and Forget: Healing the Hurts You Don't Deserve (San Francisco: Harper & Row, 1984), 52-53.

Chapter 10

1. Richard Stuart, *Helping Couples Change: A Social Learning Approach to Marital Therapy* (New York: Guilford Press, 1980), 369-372.

2. Denis Waitley, *Seeds of Greatness* (Old Tappan, NJ:Flemming Revell, 1983).

3. Harville Hendrix, *Keeping the Love You Find* (New York: Pocket Books, 1992), p. 288-291.

4. Harville Hendrix, *Getting the Love You Want* (New York: Harper Perennial, 1988), 157.

5. Janet Woititz, *The Struggle for Intimacy*, (Deerfield Beach, FL: Health Communications, 1985), 48-49.

6. *Mirroring* is a term used in Imago Therapy, *active listening* is used in Parent Effectiveness Training, and *parroting* is used in some of Gary Smalley's communication training.

7. Hendrix. *Getting*, 290.

8. Ibid., 123.

9. Stuart., 197-207

Chapter 11

1. Harville Hendrix, *Getting the Love You Want* (New York: Harper Perennial, 1988), p. 291.

2. Jeannette and Robert Lauer, "Marriages Made to Last," *Psychology Today* 19:6, (June, 1985), 85–89.

Bibliography

Brand, Paul. "The Gift of Pain." *Christianity Today*. January 1994: 18–24.

BoszormeNyi-Nag, Ivan and Geraldine Sparks. *Invisible Loyalties*. New York: Brunner Mazel, 1983.

Crabb, Larry. *Inside Out*. Colorado Springs: NavPress, 1988.

Gottman, John. *The Marriage Clinic*. New York: W.W. Norton, 1999.

Harlow, Harry. *Learning to Love*. New York: Janson Aronson, 1974.

Hendrix, Harville. *Getting the Love You Want*. New York: Harper Perennial, 1990.

Hendrix, Harville. *Keeping the Love You Find*. New York: Pocket Books, 1992.

Lauer, Jeanette and Robert. "Marriages Made to Last." *Psychology Today*. June 1985: 85–89.

Love, Patricia. *The Emotional Incest Syndrome*. New York: Bantam, 1990.

Moore, Thomas. *The Care of the Soul*. New York: Harper Perennial, 1994.

Ornstein, Robert and David Sobel. *The Healing Brain*. New York: Simon and Schuster, 1987.

Rodgers, Beverly and Tom. *Adult Children of Divorced Parents: Making Your Marriage Work*. San Jose: Resource Publications, 2002.

Sanford, John. *Invisible Partners*. New York: Paulist Press, 1980.

Sanford, John and Paula. *The Transformation of the Inner Man*. New York: Bridge Publishers, 1982.

Seamands, David. *Healing Damaged Emotions*. Wheaton: Victor Books, 1983.

Smedes, Lewis. *Forgive and Forget*. San Francisco: Harper and Row, 1984.

Springle, Pat. *Close Enough to Care*. Dallas: Rapha/Word, 1990.

Stuart, Richard. *Helping Couples Change: A Social Learning Approach to Marital Therapy*. New York: Guilford Press, 1980.

Tennov, Dorothy. *Love and Limerance: The Experience of Being in Love*. New York: Stein and Day, 1979.

Toufexis, Anastasia. The Right Chemistry. Time. February 5, 1993: 48-51.

Waitley, Dennis. *Seeds of Greatness*. Old Tappan: Fleming Revell, 1993.

Warren, Neil Clark. *Finding the Love of Your Life: Ten Principles for Choosing the Right Marriage Partner*. New York: Pocket Books, 1992.

Woititz, Janet. Stuggle for Intimacy. Deerfield Beach, FL.: Health Communications, 1985.

Appendix

The Forgiving Experience

Step 1

Sender (the Offended Partner): Ask for a time to share.

Receiver (the Offender): Grant the request for a time ASAP. In truth, either the offender or the offended partner can ask for a time to share, and they both agree on a time as soon as possible.

Step 2

Sender: List all of the offenses your partner has committed—how he or she has hurt you and how you feel. Give it all of the emotion it deserves (with no tissue damage, property damage, or soul damage).

Receiver: Put on your spiritual and psychic armor and become a "container" for your mate's anger.

Step 3

Sender: The Explosion—Give it the anger it deserves.

Receiver: Listen with empathy and *koinonia.*

Step 4

Sender: The Implosion—allow the anger to soak in and turn to tears.

Receiver: Provide support, listen with empathy, and allow a natural pause so that the couple can collect themselves and continue.

Receiver takes the lead and Sender listens.

Step 5

Receiver: Take the lead and admit your actions with empathy by verbally acknowledging that you hurt your partner and what you did to do this.

Sender: Listen and absorb.

Step 6

Receiver: Describe with empathy how your spouse must feel about the hurt you caused.

Sender: Listen and absorb.

Step 7

Receiver: Reverently request your partner's forgiveness. Ask the question, "Would you, could you, ever find it in your heart to forgive me for what I have done to you?"

Sender: Grant the request for your partner's forgiveness as best you can at the time and commit to work on forgiving that which you cannot presently forgive.

Step 8

Receiver: List how you will commit to never do those hurtful things again. List the things you will do to make these changes.

Sender: Share things that your partner can do to change. Express gratitude and appreciation.

About The Institute for Soul-Healing Love

Marriages are ending in record numbers and Christian marriages are no exception. Not only that, the nation's singles population is growing older and larger because singles are delaying marriage or not marrying at all. These individuals and couples need help to see that long term, healthy marriage is attainable. The mission of the Institute for Soul-Healing Love is to accomplish this arduous task.

Established in 1999, the Institute for Soul-Healing Love is recognized as an international resource for churches and organizations to equip singles, couples, and leaders to develop relationships that heal. The vision of the Institute is twofold. First, it is to provide workshops for individuals and couples who want to allow God's unconditional love to heal their past hurts in order to develop healing relationships and live more healthy lives. Secondly, the vision is to train counselors, pastors, lay ministers, marriage ministers and anyone who wants to learn how to help others use the Soul-Healing Love Model. The Institute Certifies individuals to be Soul-Healers so that they can teach God's unconditional soul healing love to others. The results are marriages that bring about understanding, enhance empathy, foster forgiveness and thus heal the souls of each person as well as the soul of the marriage. If you would like to learn more visit us at www.SoulHealingLove for details.

Institute for Soul-Healing Love
E-mail: info@SoulHealingLove.com
Website:www.SoulHealingLove.com
Phone: 704 364-9176
Fax: 704 366-0729

Address:
1206 Jules Ct.
Charlotte, NC 28226

Resources for Building Healthy Relationships

Soul-Healers Leaders Guide
A step-by-step process for using Soul-Healing Love with your group or organization.

**Soul-Healers Workshop
on DVD**
10 hrs of a Soul-Healers Workshop in a 3 DVD set.

"I highly endorse the speaking and writing ministry of Drs. Bev and Tom Rodgers." Les Parrott, Author and Speaker, Founder and Director of the Center for Real Relationships, and Professor of Clinical Psychology Seattle Pacific University.

To order these materials call 704-364-9176 or visit
www.SoulHealingLove.com

Resources for Building Healthy Relationships

2.5 hr. Highlight of Soul-Healers Workshop with Workbook

13 lessons which include all 10 exercises

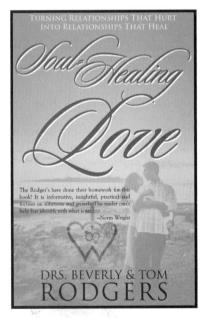

Soul-Healing Love Book on CD

Listen to Drs. Bev and Tom in your car or while you work.

To order these materials call 704-364-9176 or visit
www.SoulHealingLove.com